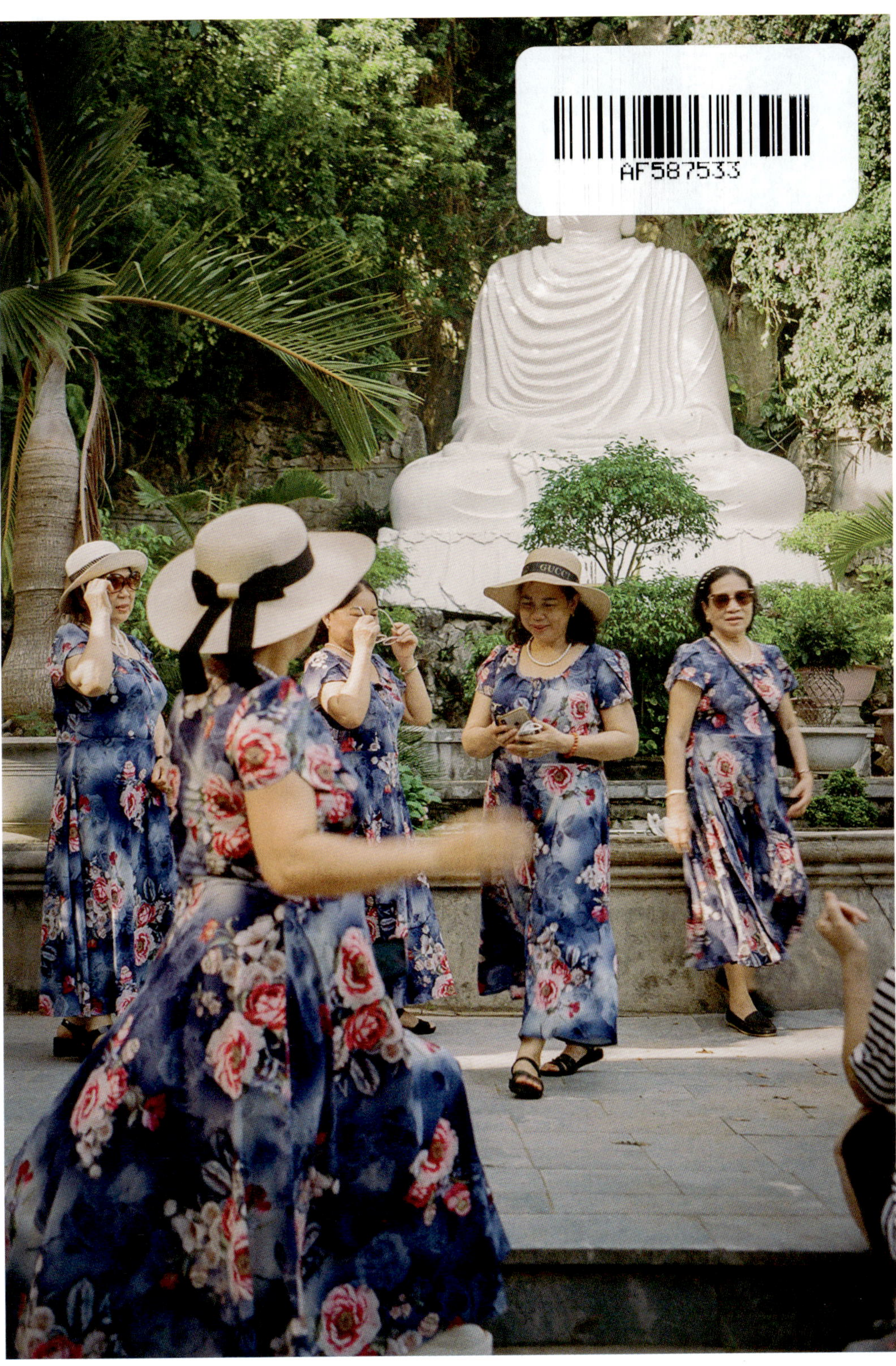
GUCCI

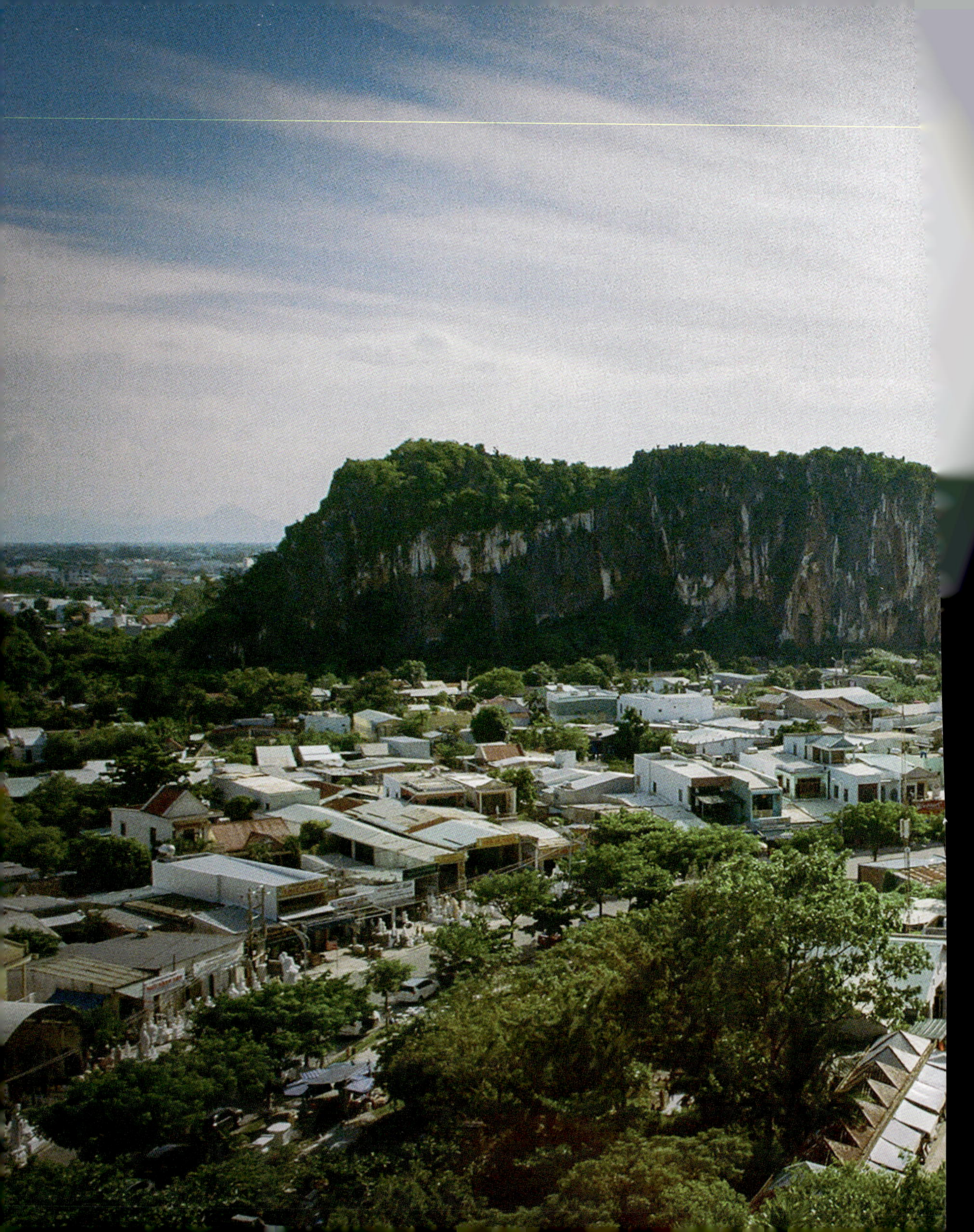

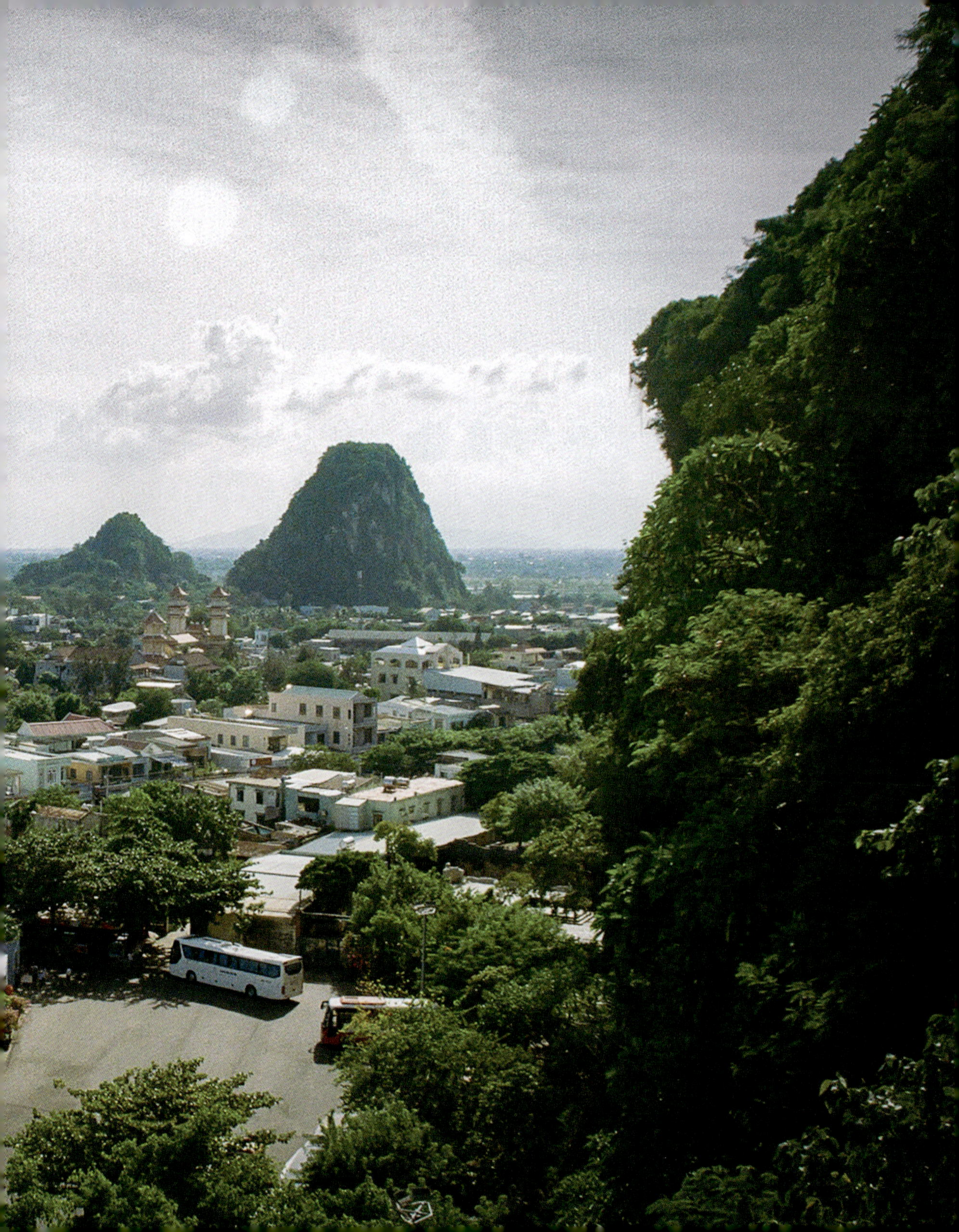

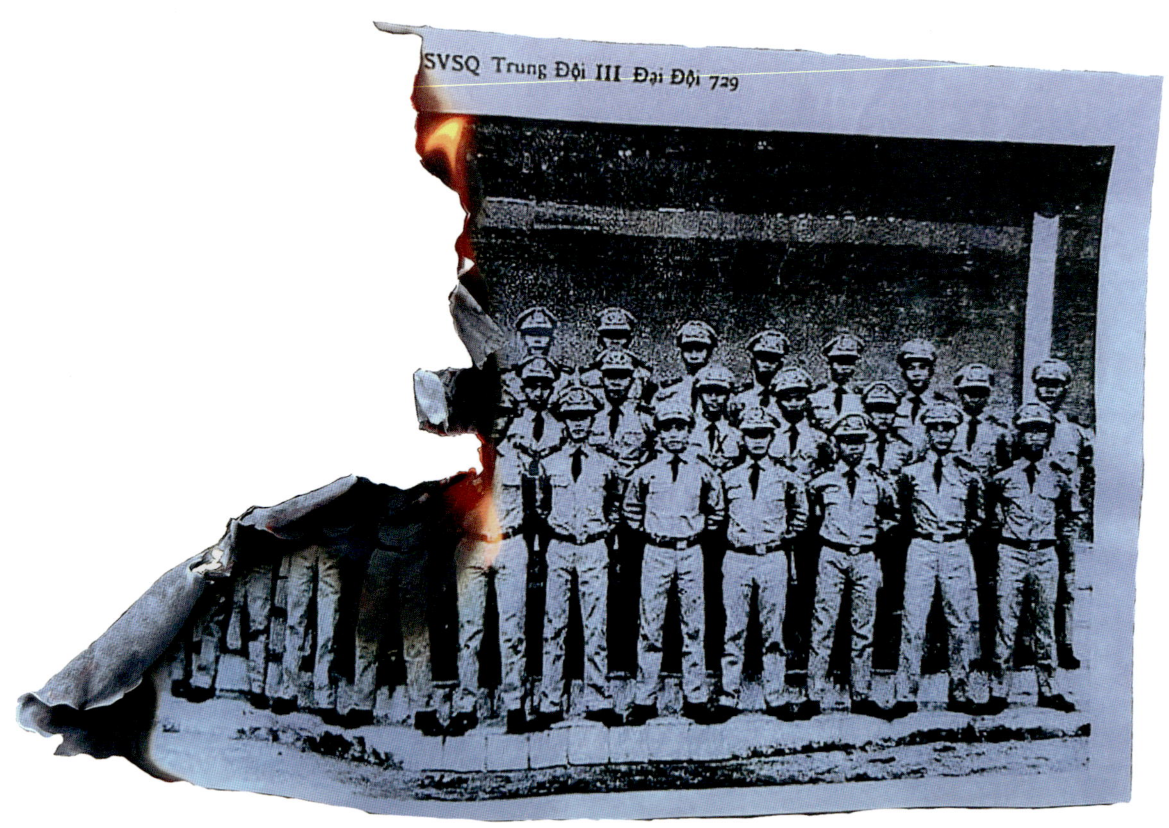
SVSQ Trung Đội III Đại Đội 729

“What happened to you after the war ended?”

“After April 30, 1975, the North took over South Vietnam. I was forced into a detention camp for 3 years. I was given only one suit of clothes for my whole time there, a brown and white striped prisoner uniform. Most of my work was to cut down trees and transport lumber. At times we’d have to cross rivers where the water would reach my chest. I’d dry my only set of clothes in my tent. We were treated worse than prisoners. When I was released in 1978, my life did not return to normal, as the new government treated me differently because of my history as an officer. I had to report to the government day and night of my daily activities. I had my valuables confiscated. I could not find work, I had to use my mother’s last name to work secretly at a soap factory. I had to burn the photos and any record of myself of who I was in the war. I saved up gold that I earned at the factory to use as a bribe to escape the country by boat. Finally, in 1989, after 5 attempts, me, your mother and sister escaped on a boat with 135 other people.”

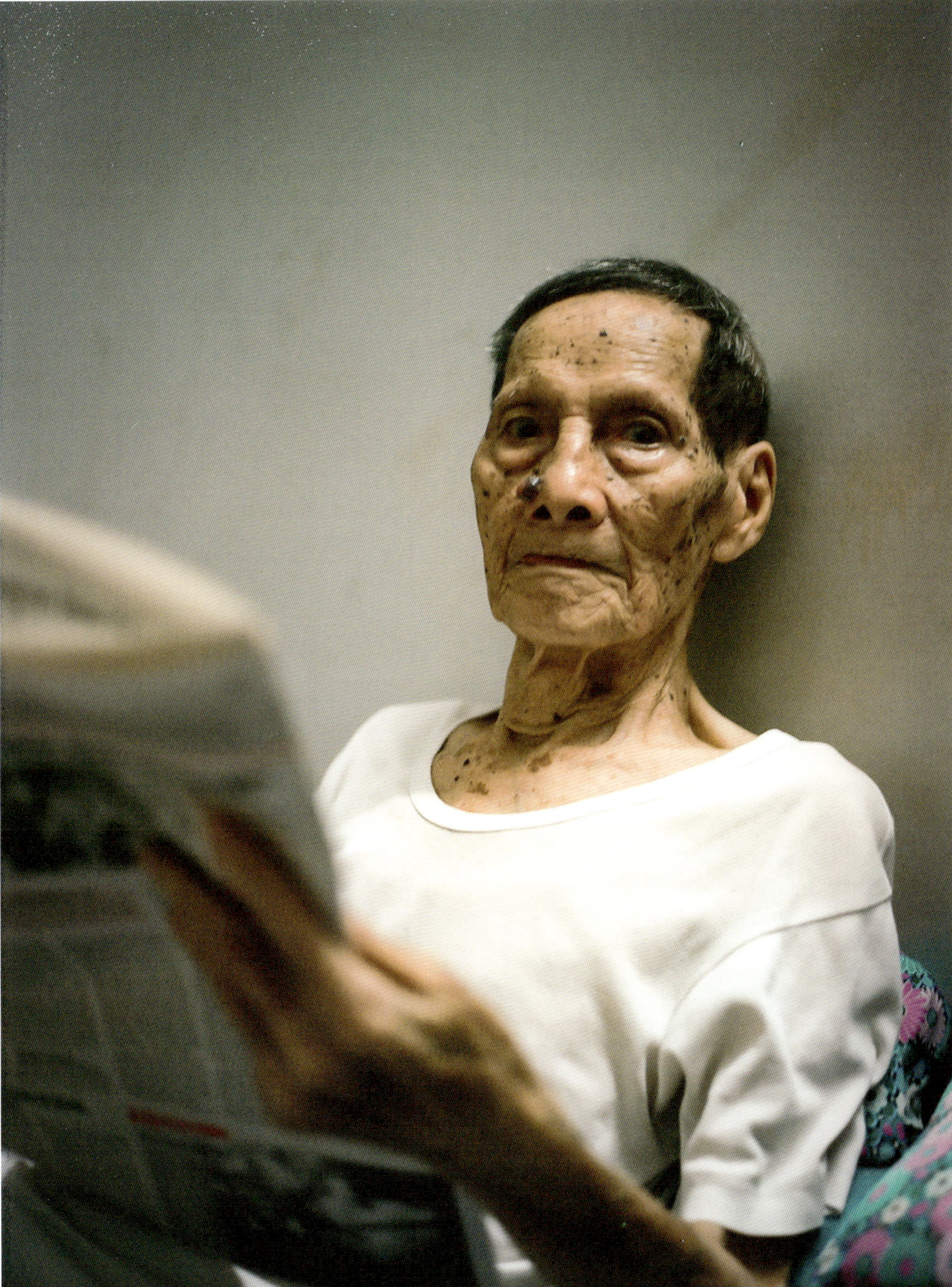

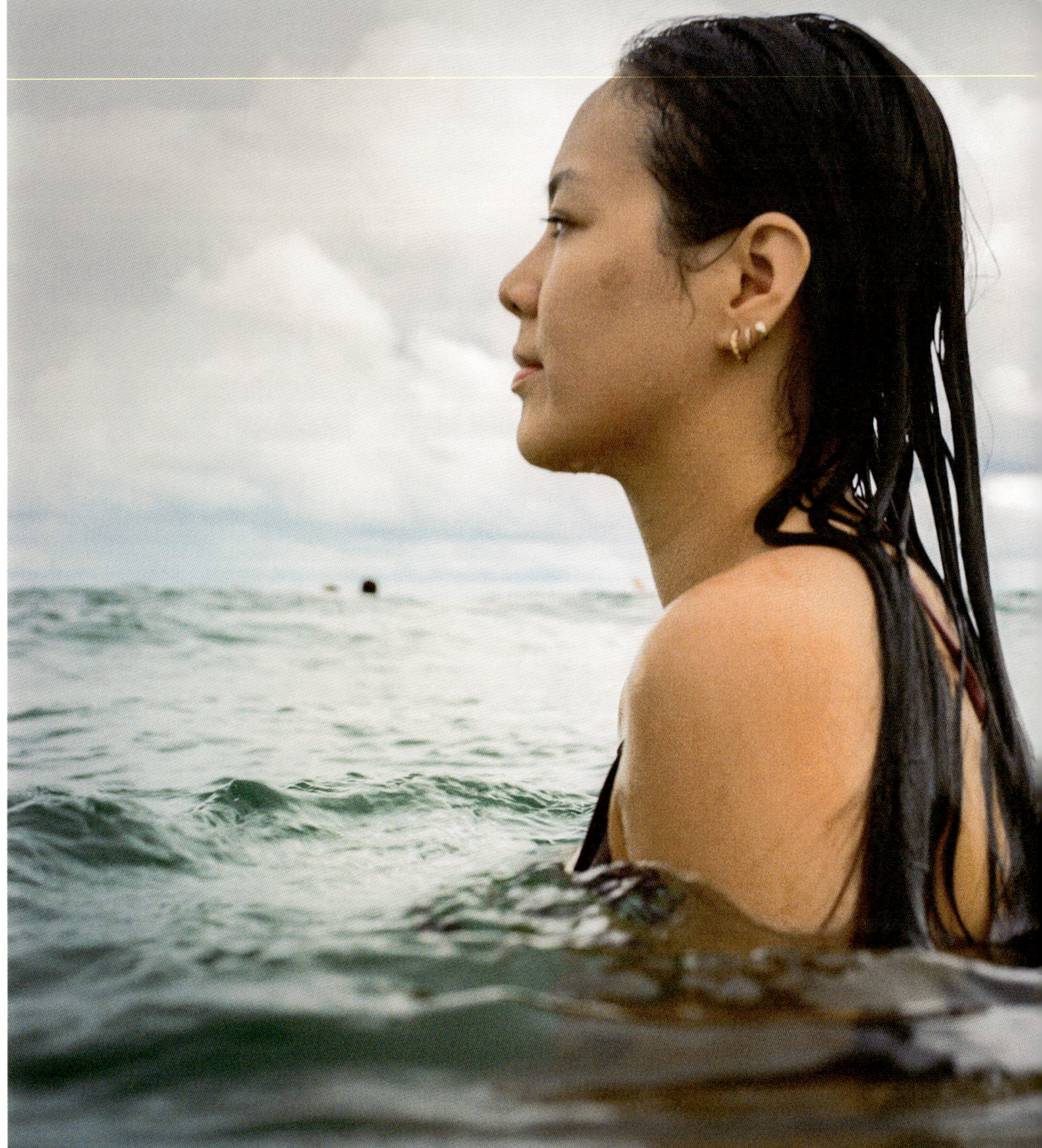

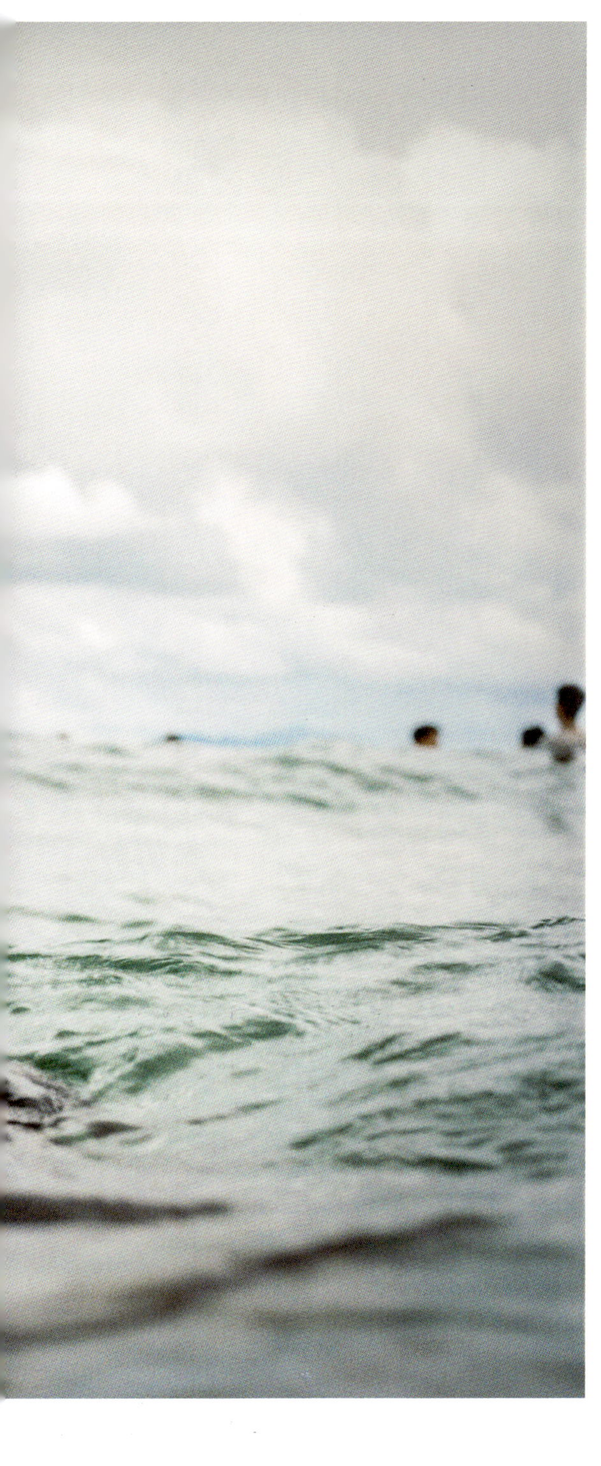

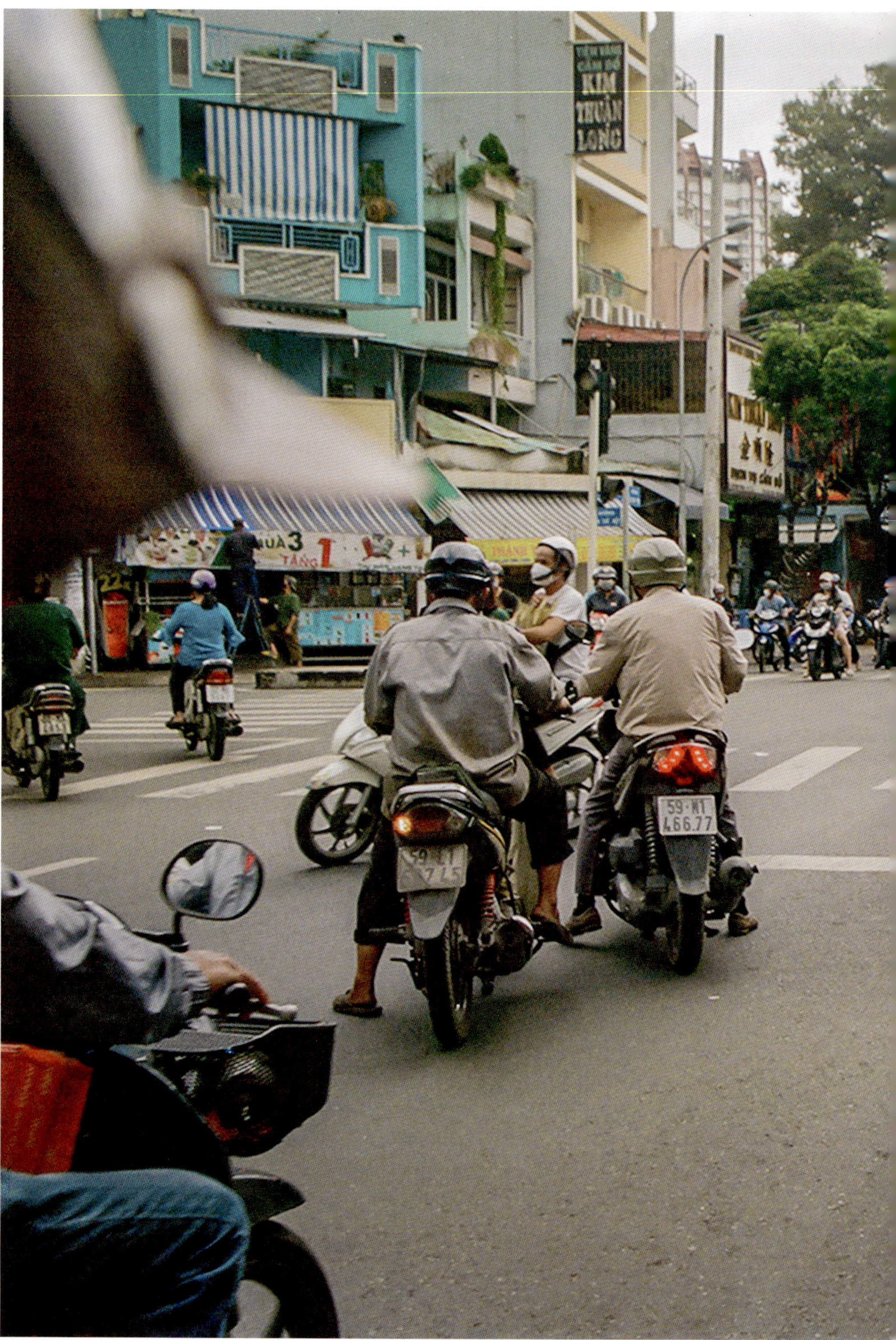
KIM
THUẬN
LONG
TẶNG 1
466.77

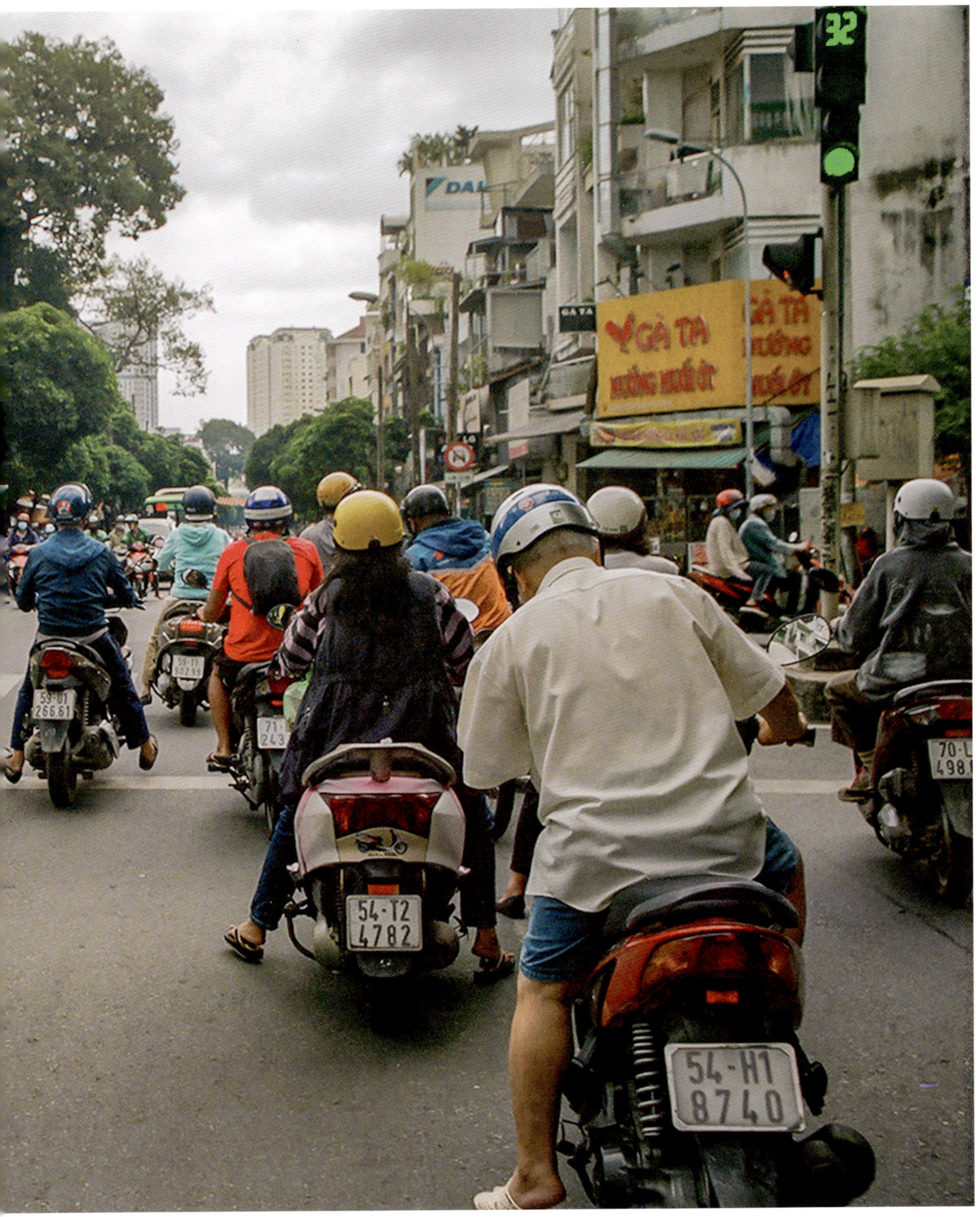

GÀ TA
NƯỚNG MUỐI ỚT
54-T2
4782
54-H1
8740

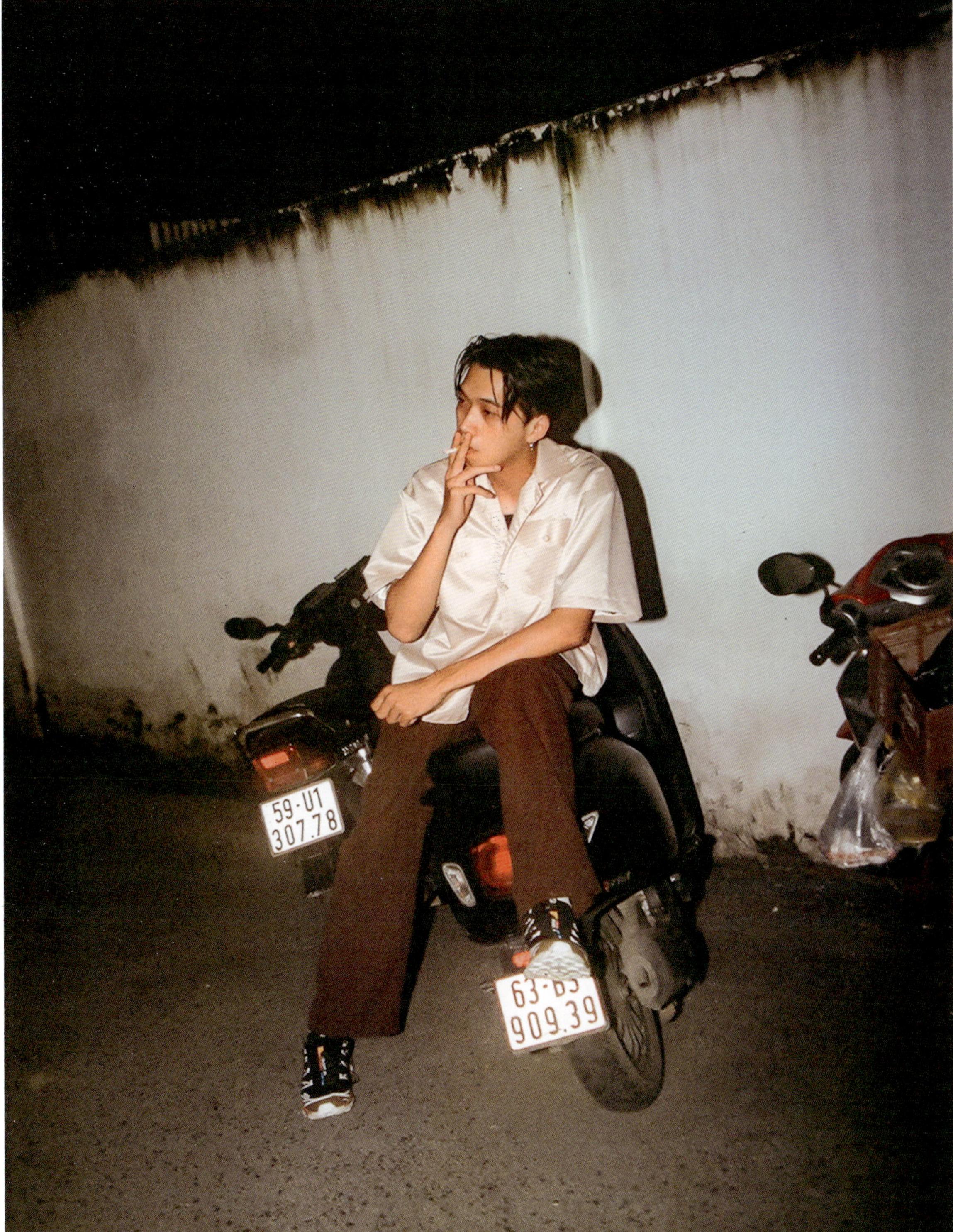
59-U1
307.78
909.39

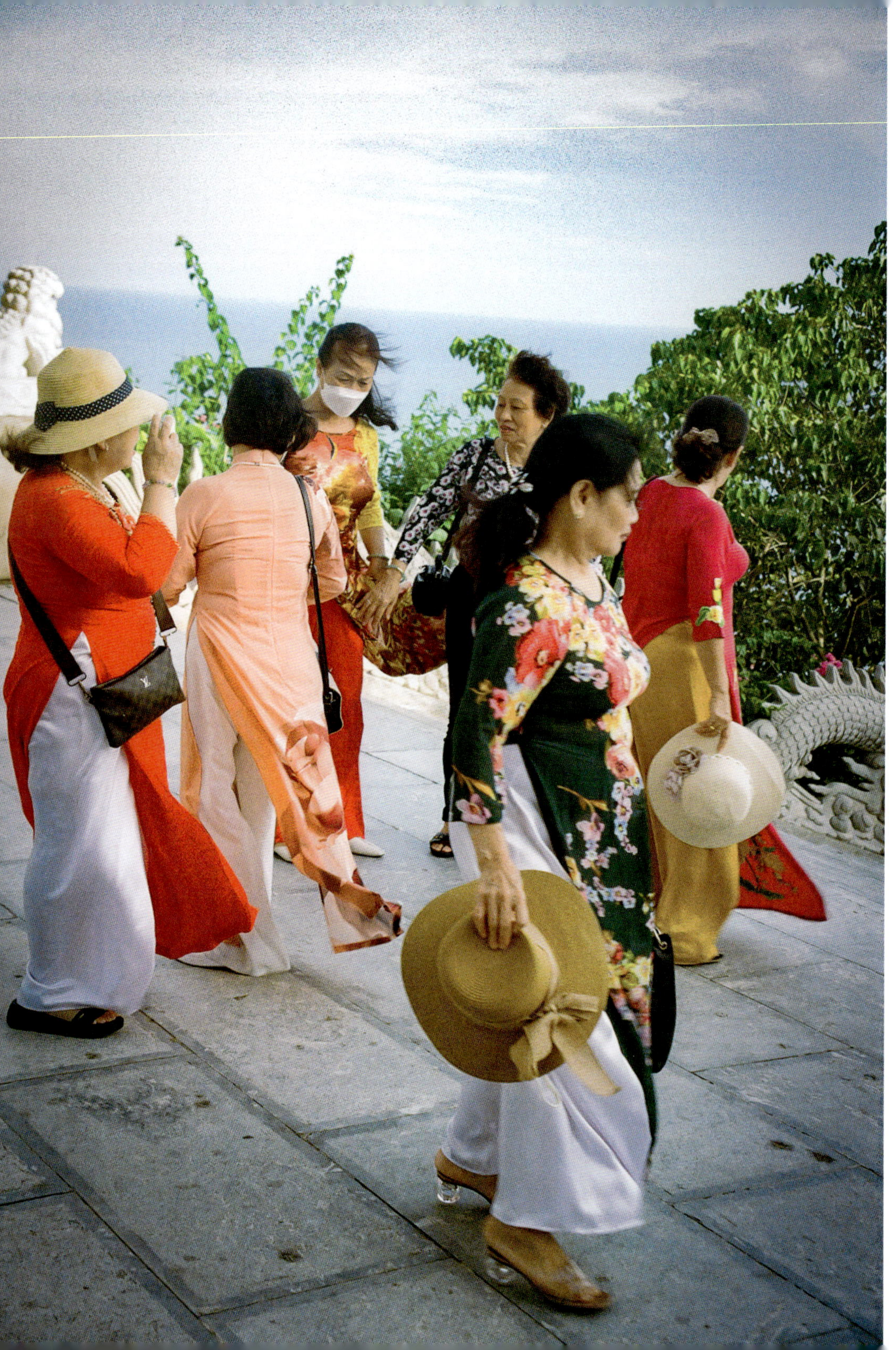

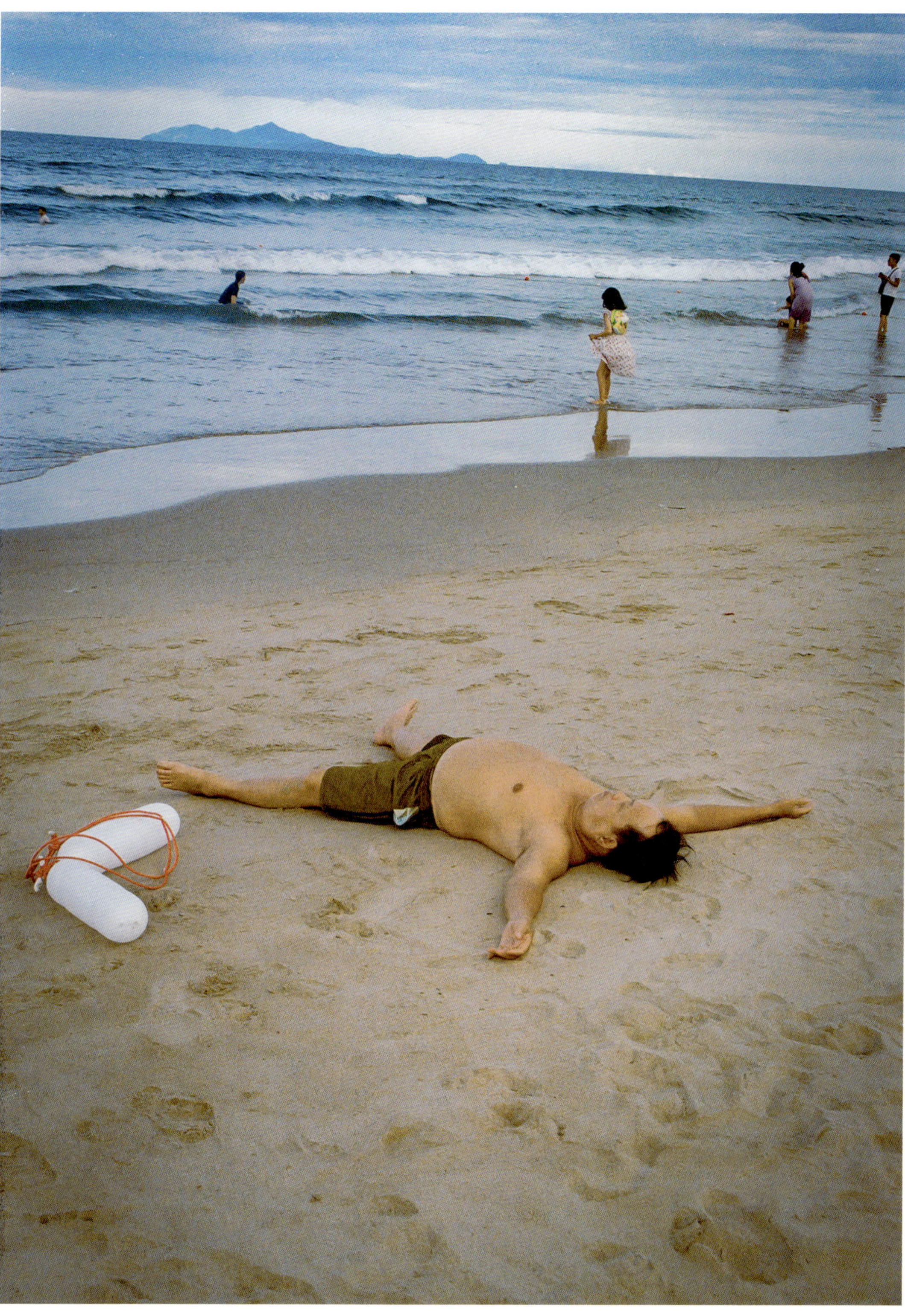

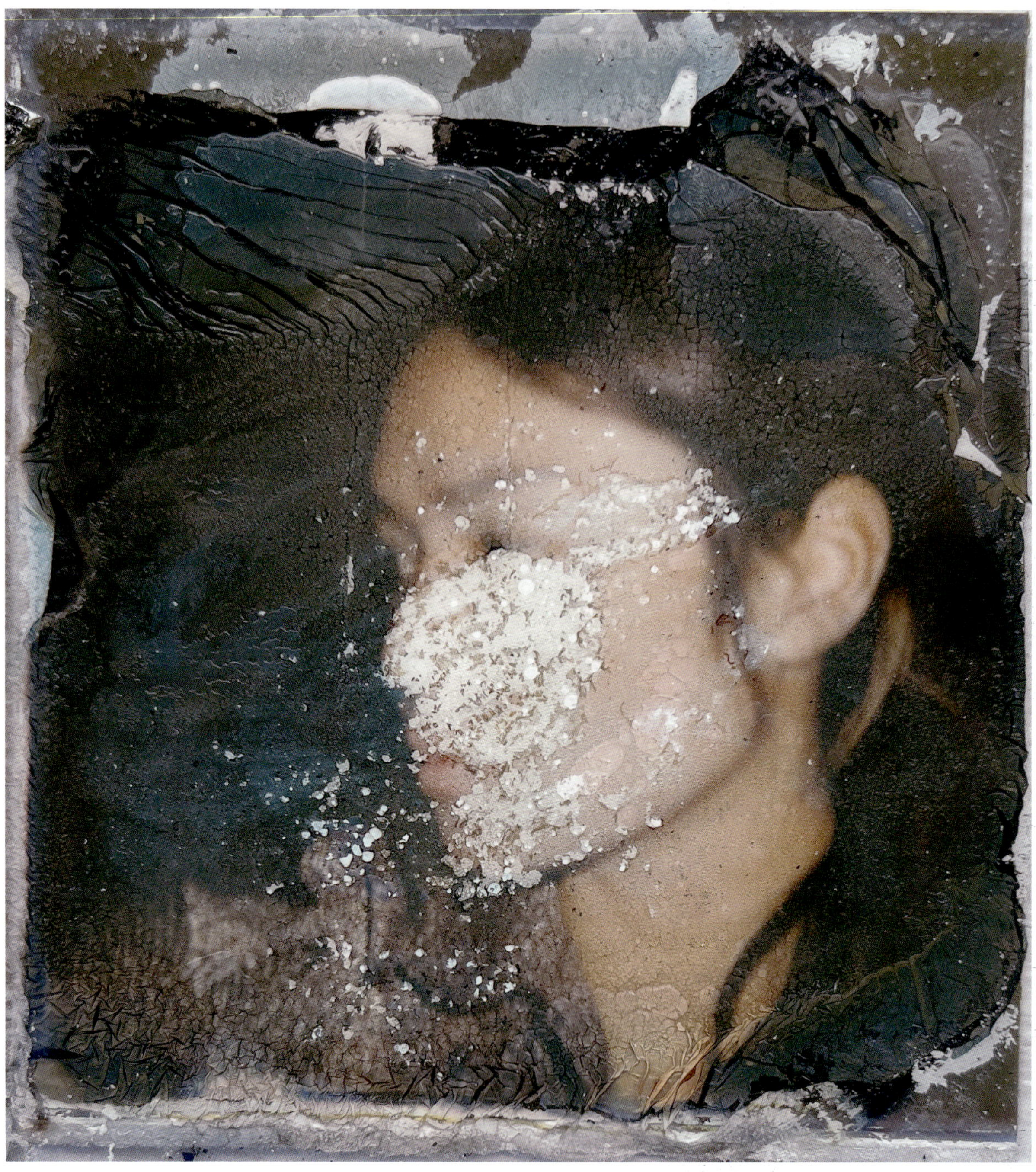

IS SELF LIBERATION ACHIEVED WITH
OR WITHOUT MUTUAL PROCESS?
WHAT DOES IT MEAN TO COME TO
TRANSCEDENT IDENTITY IN A
COUNTRY MARKED BY WAR?
DISPLACED, REVIVED, LOST, RESCINDED
I DIDN'T MEAN TO LEAVE YOU BEHIND
I HAVE ASSIMILATED TO A NAME
THAT WAS NEVER MINE
I MIGHT HAVE REMORSE BUT OUR
HONEY DRIPS FROM THE SAME
CASE OF OPPRESSION
I'VE COME BACK TO RECLAIM
BUT TO WHAT AM I RECLAIMING?
TO LOVE IS TO ANATOMIZE THE SELF

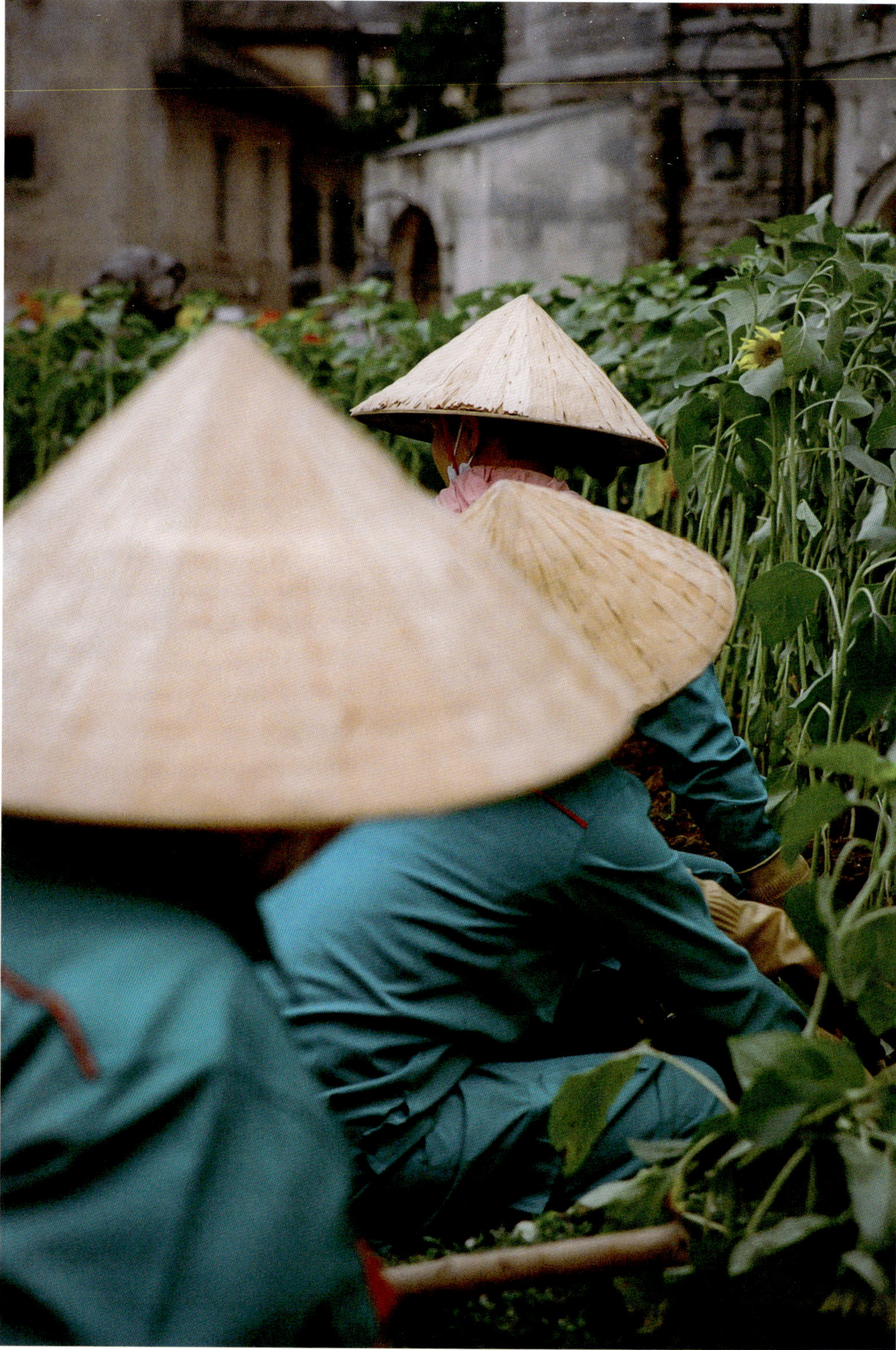

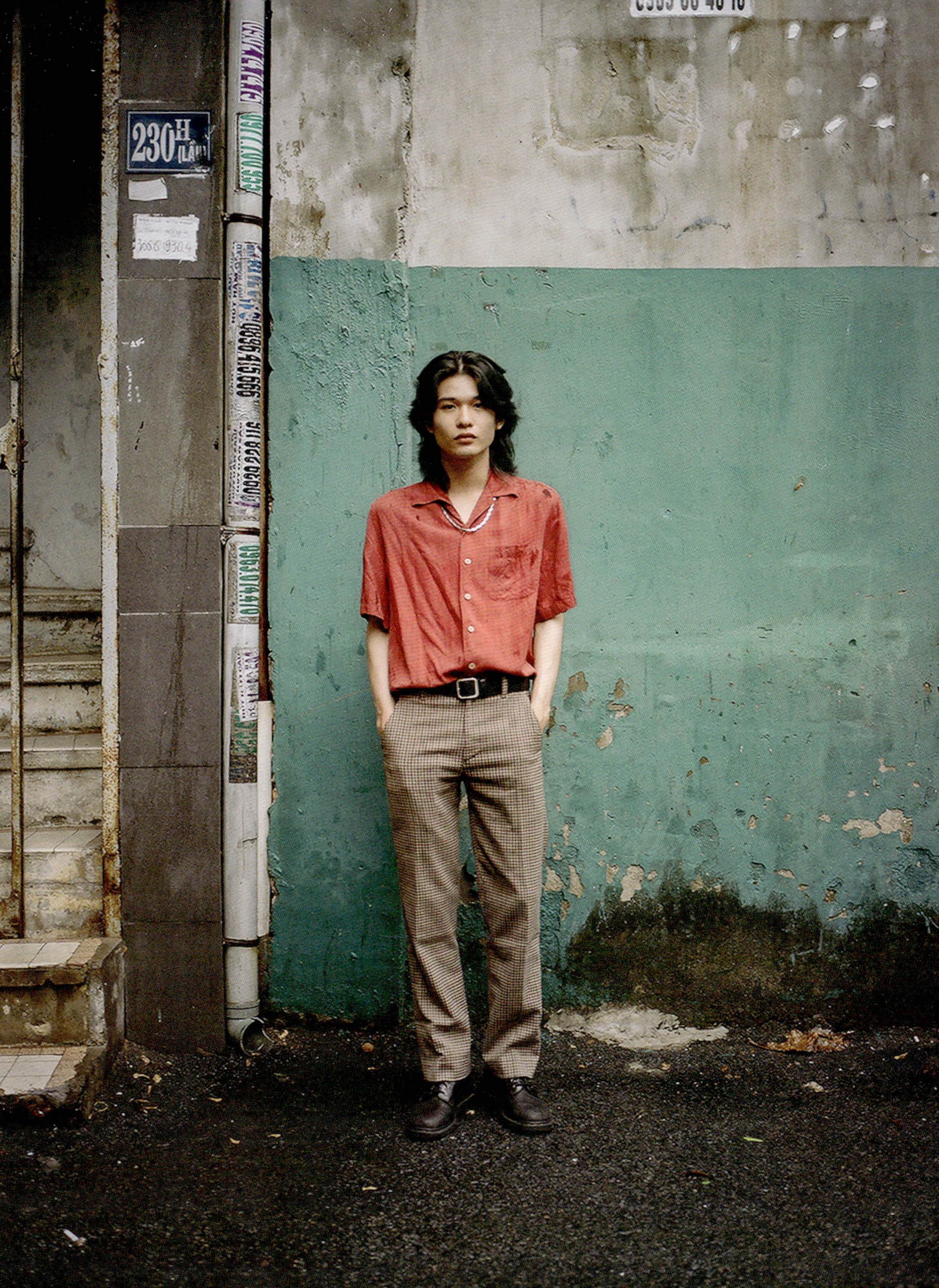
230H

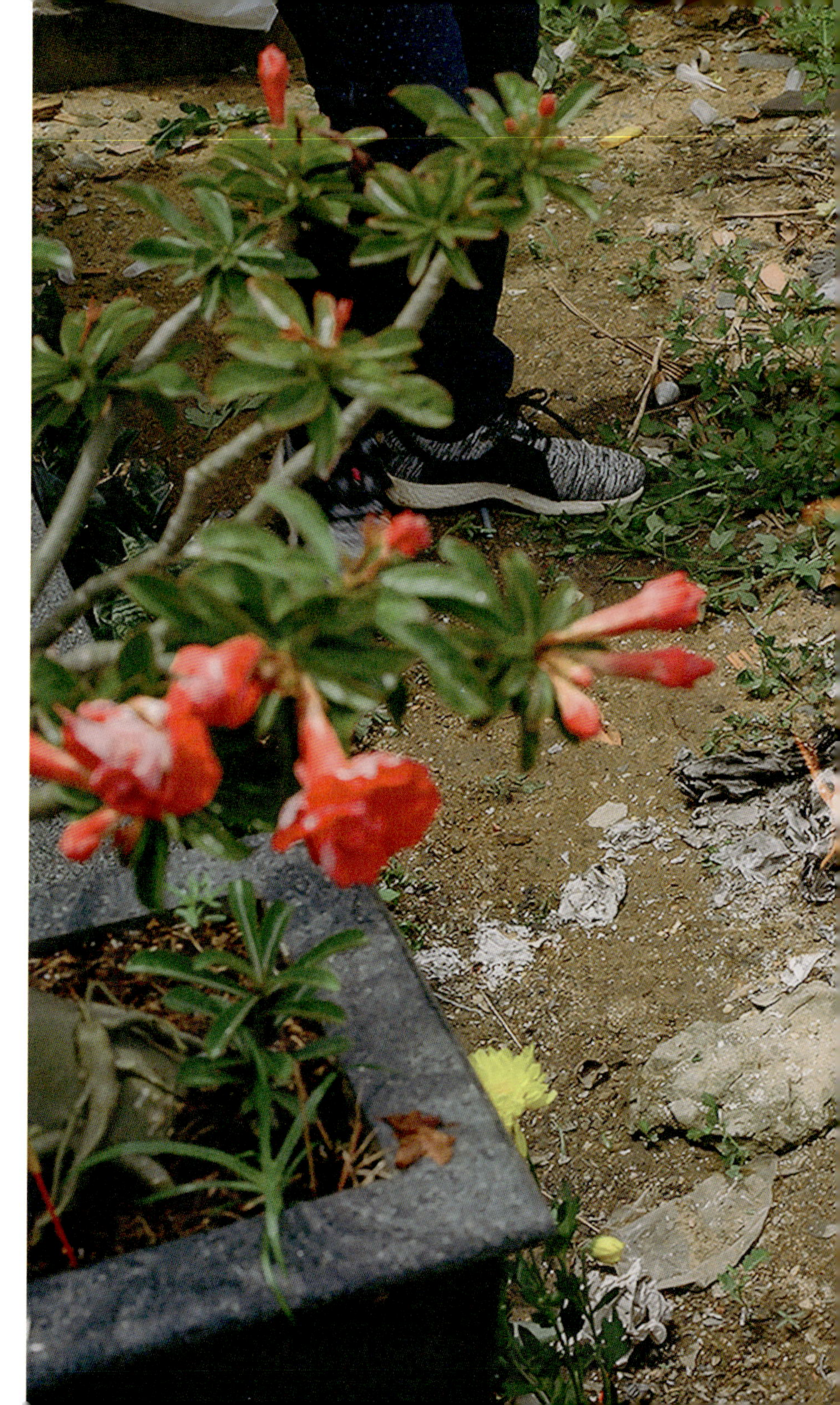

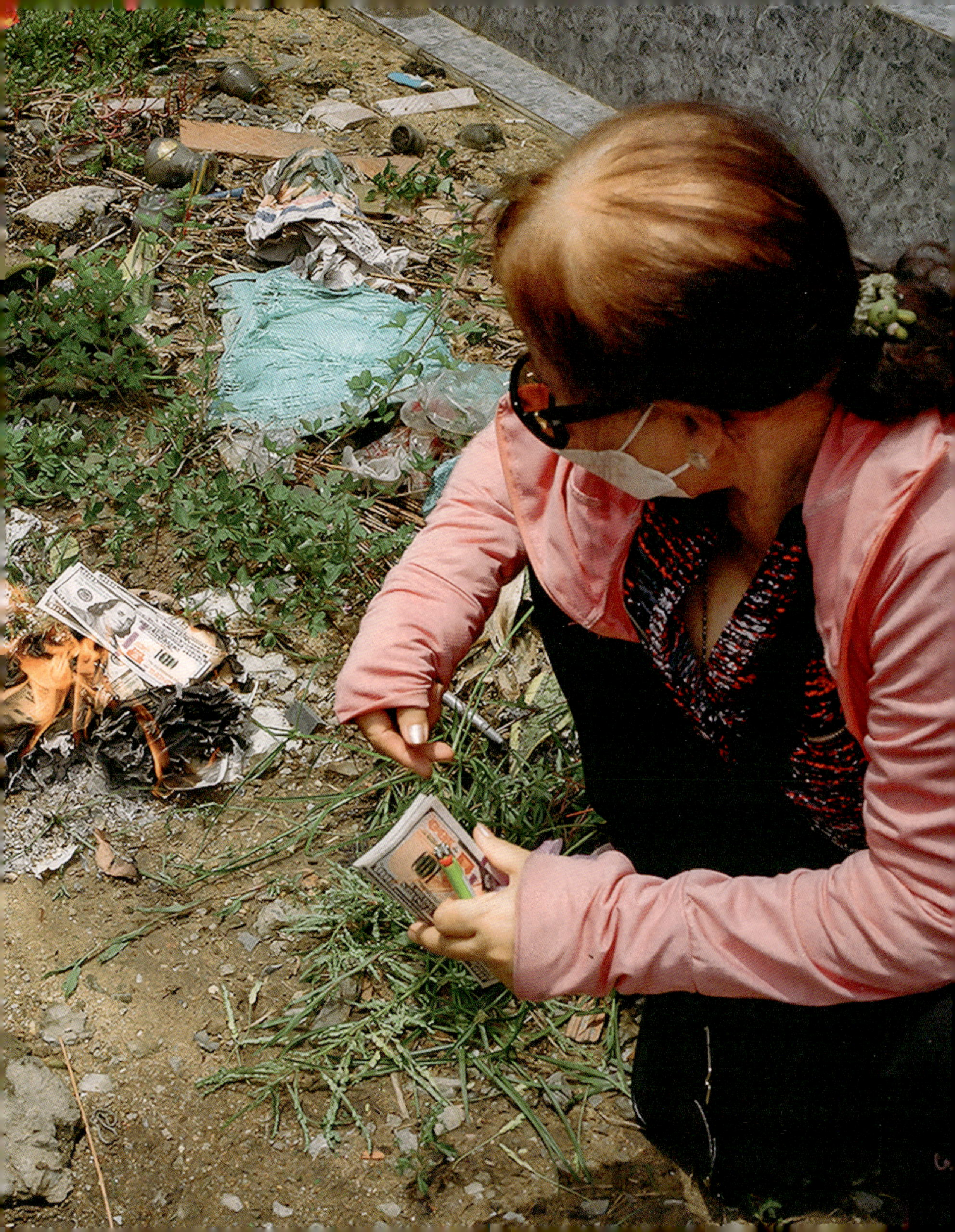

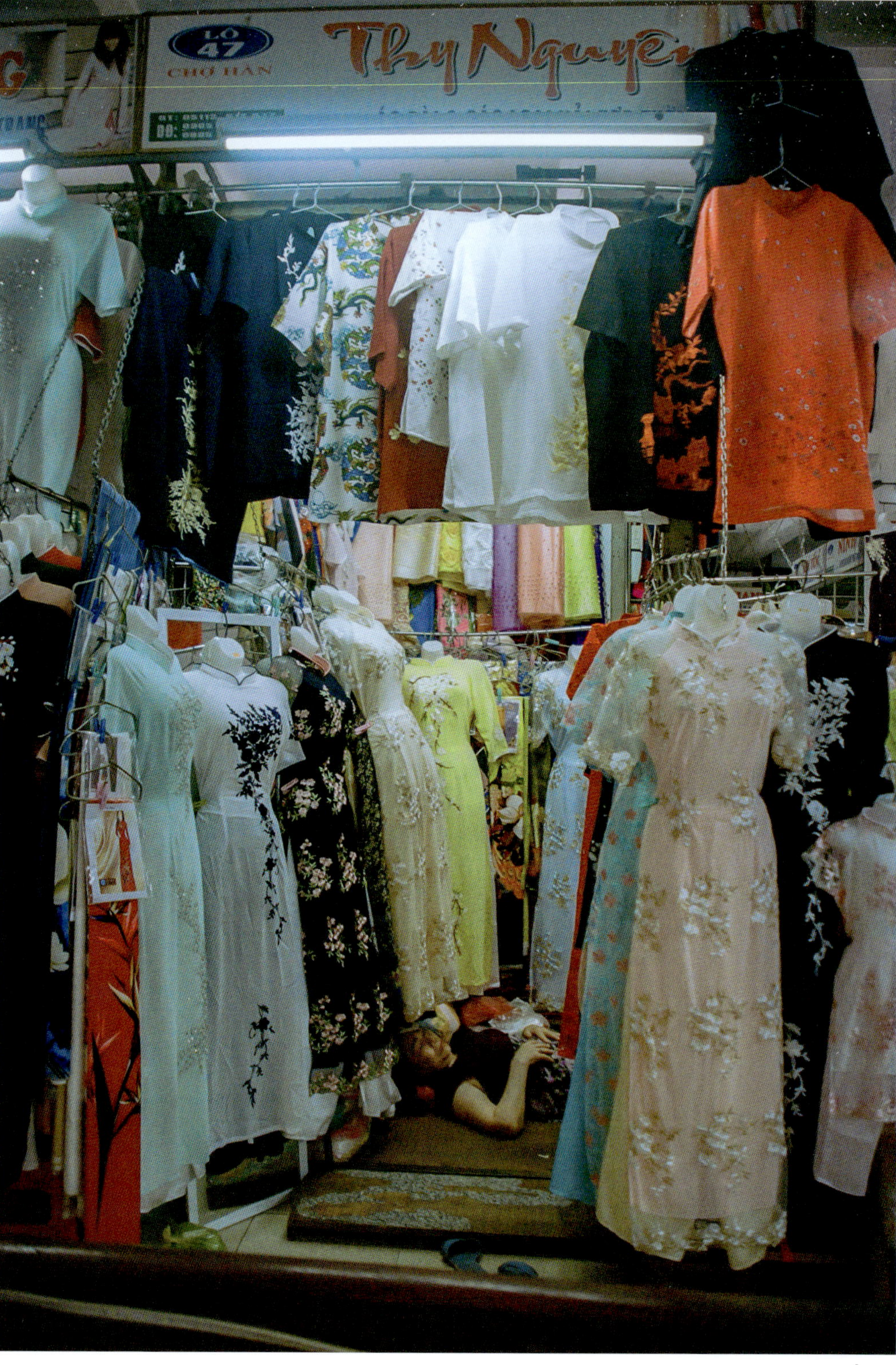
LÔ 47
CHỢ HÀN
Thy

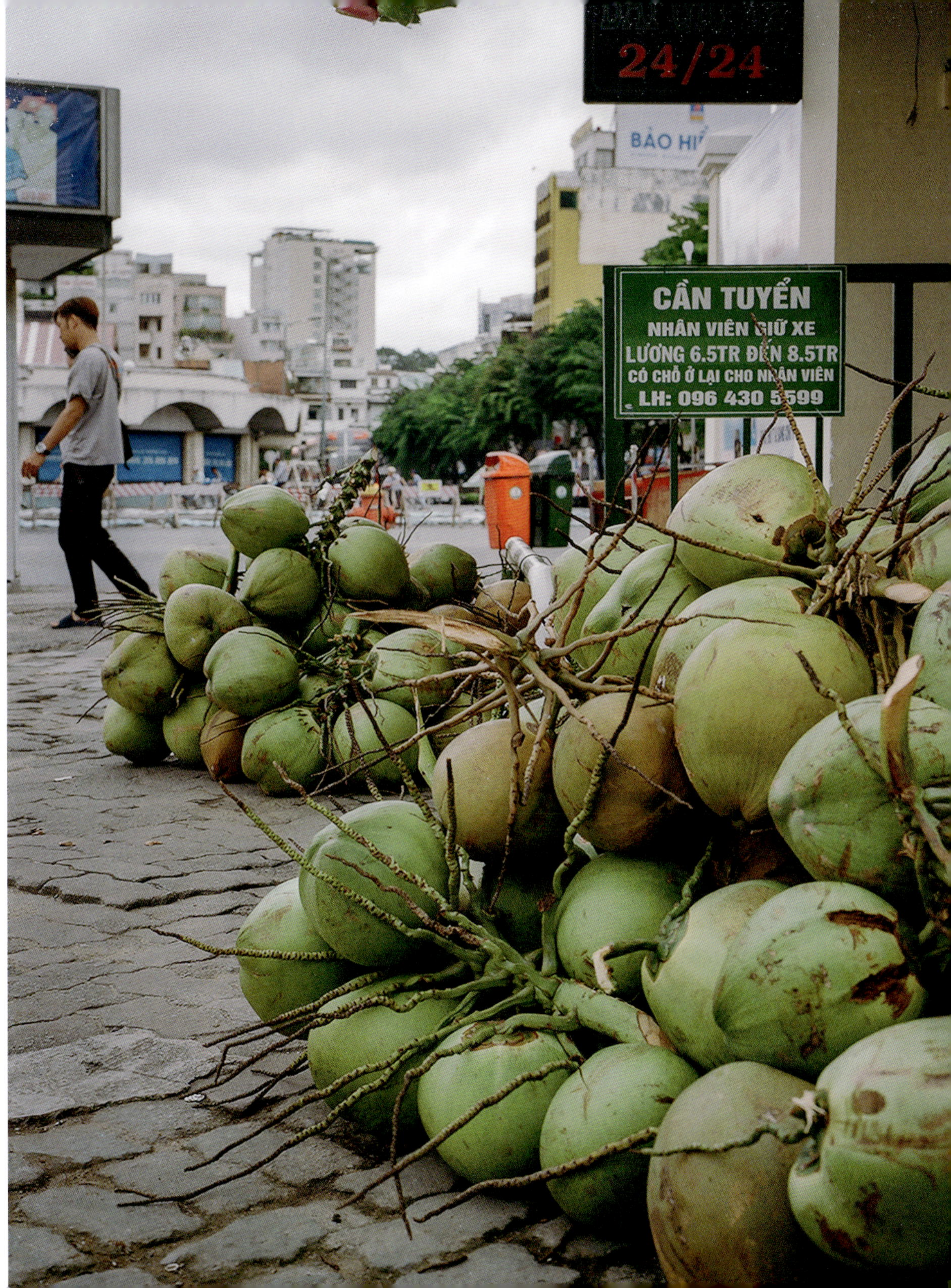
24/24
CẦN TUYỂN
NHÂN VIÊN GIỮ XE
LƯƠNG 6.5TR ĐẾN 8.5TR
CÓ CHỖ Ở LẠI CHO NHÂN VIÊN
LH: 096 430 5599

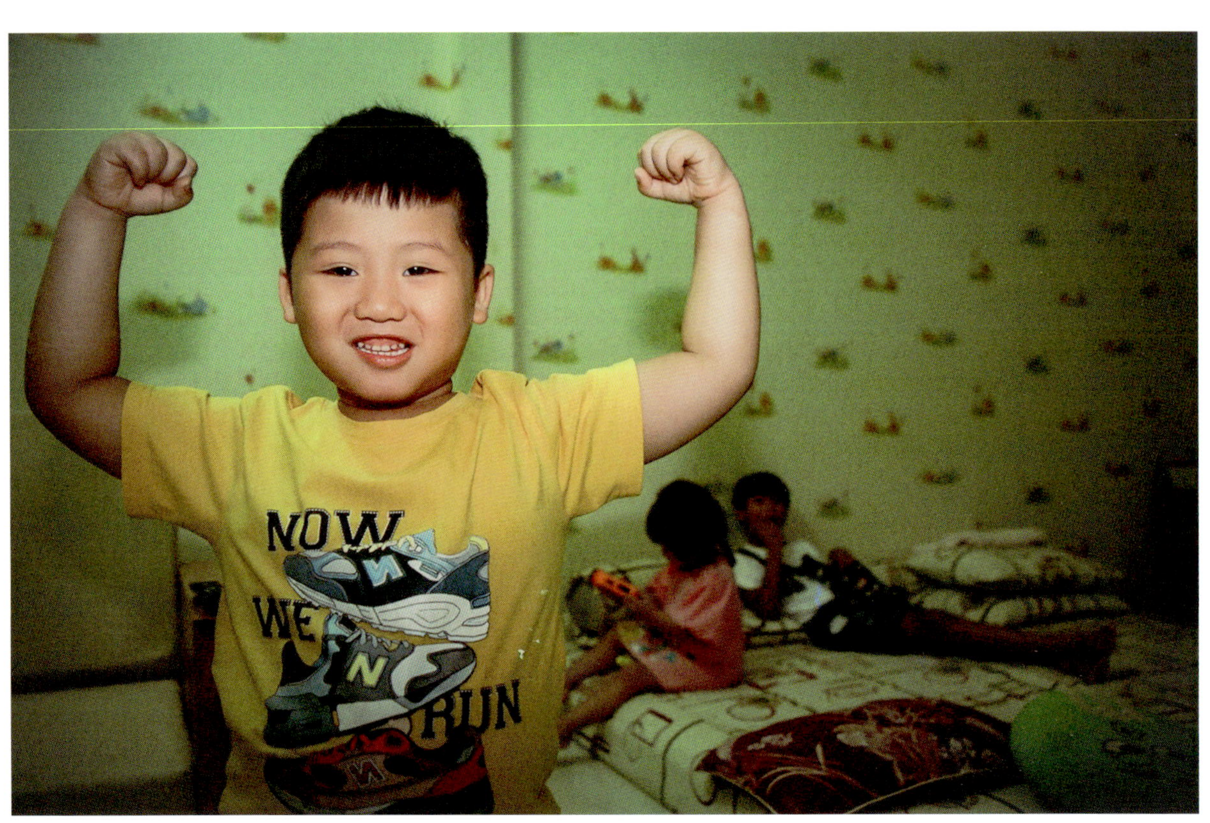
NOW
WE
RUN

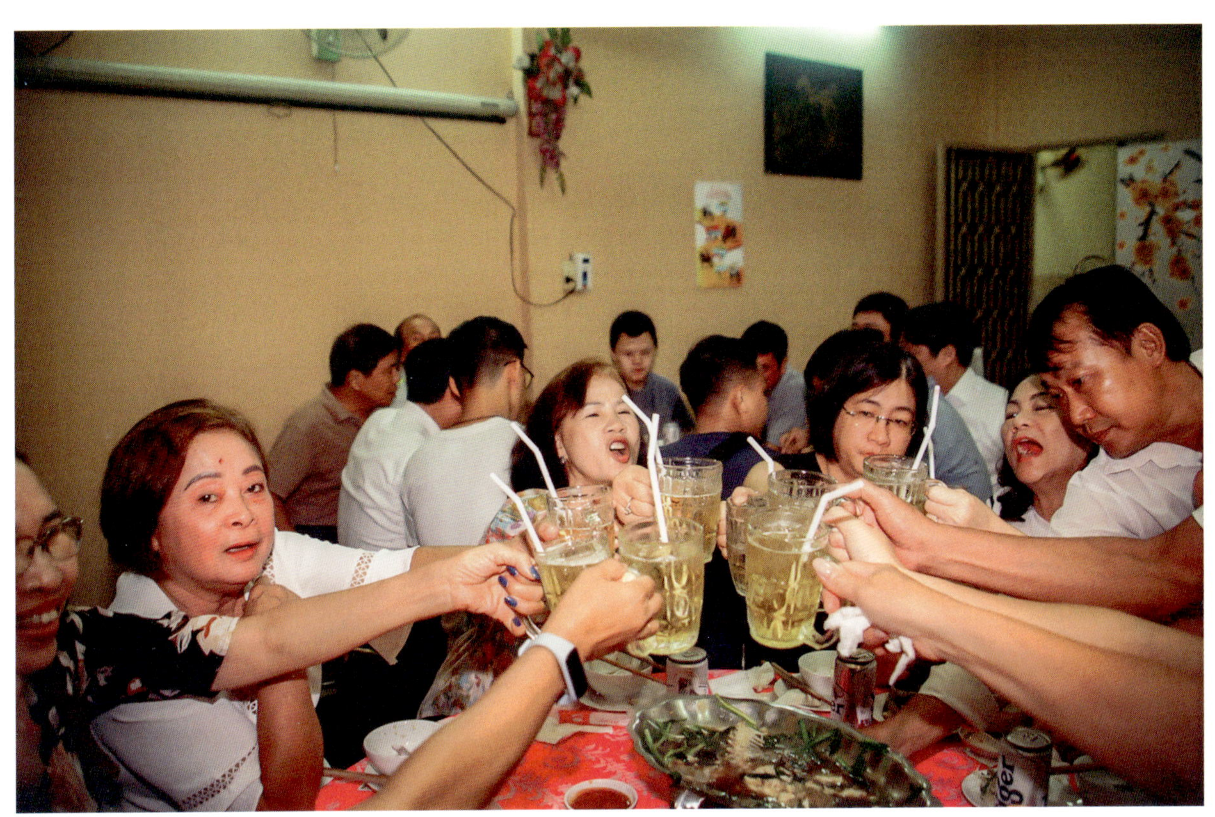

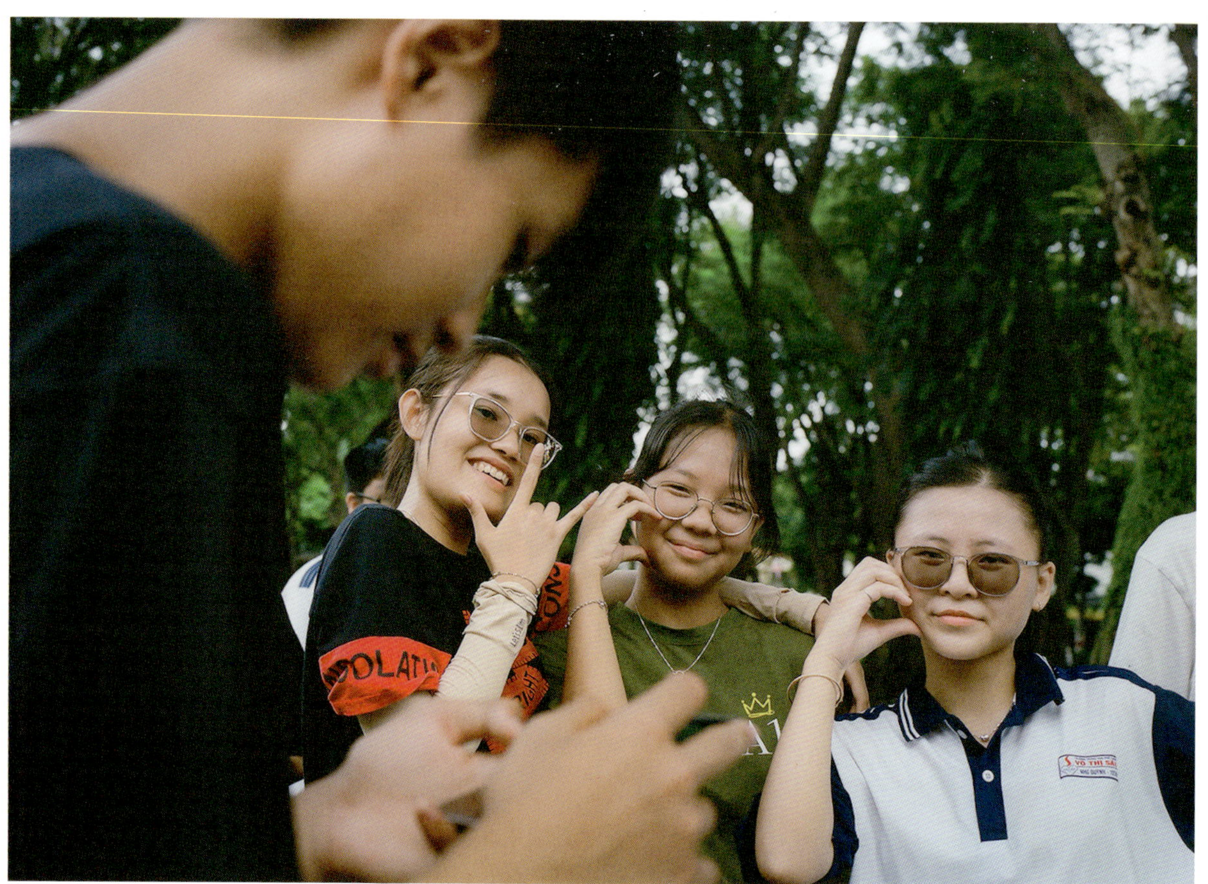

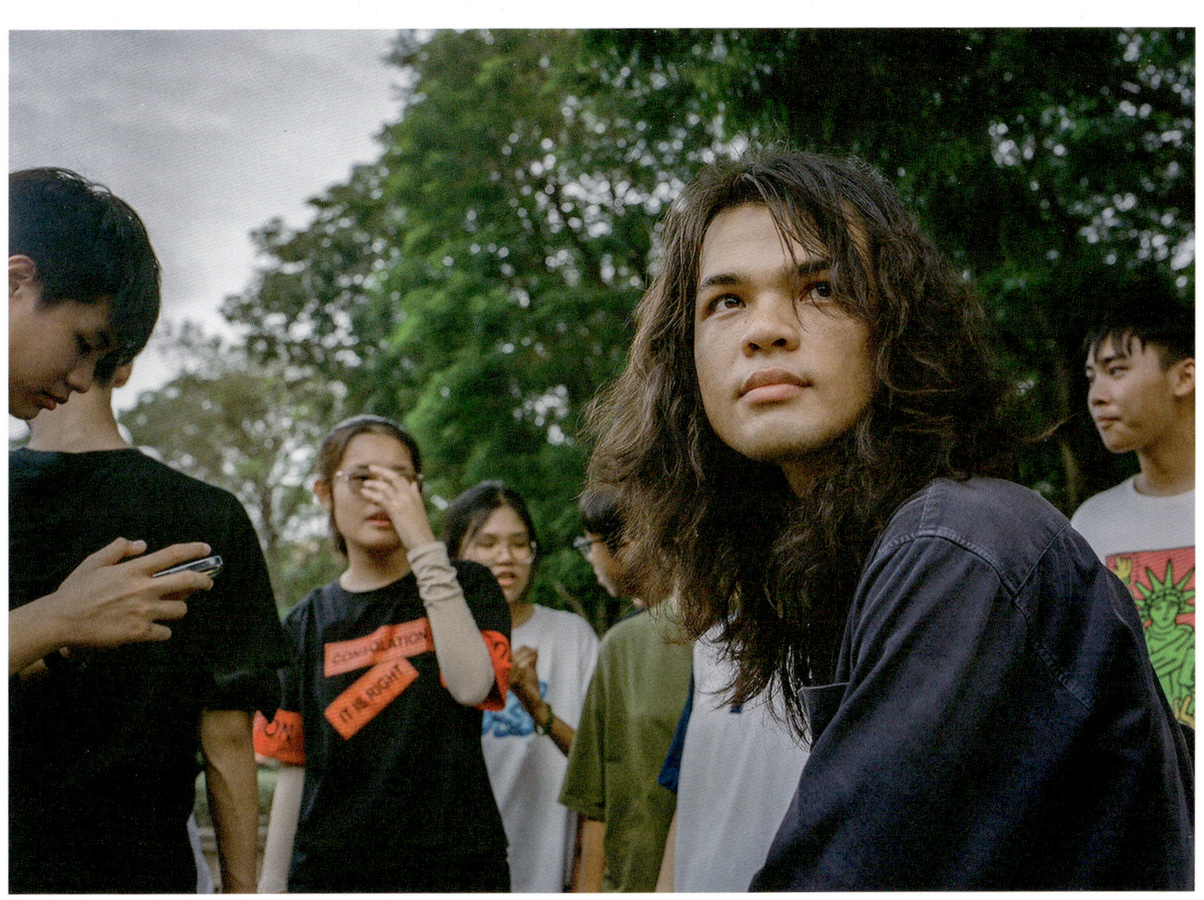
IT IS RIGHT

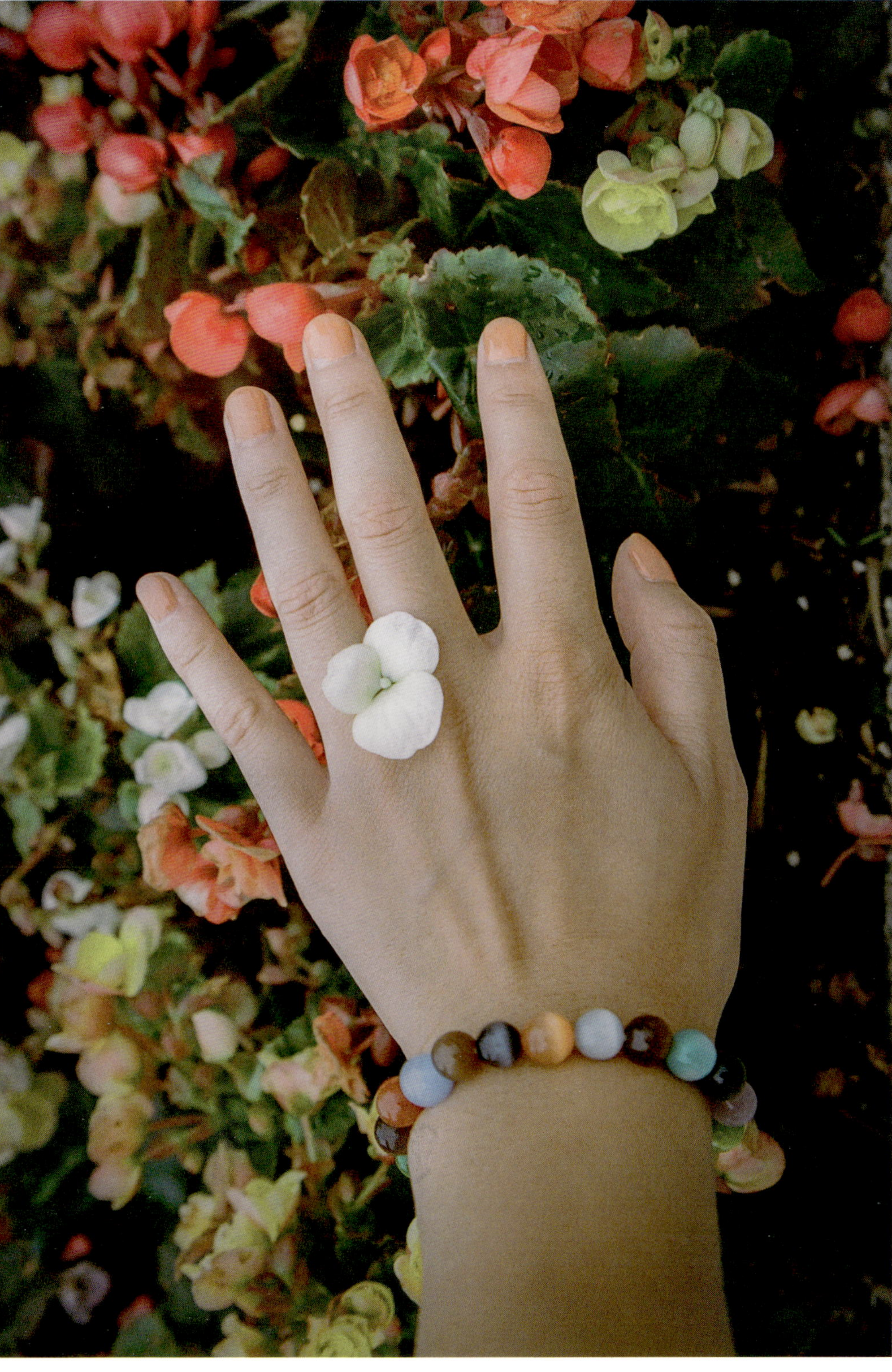

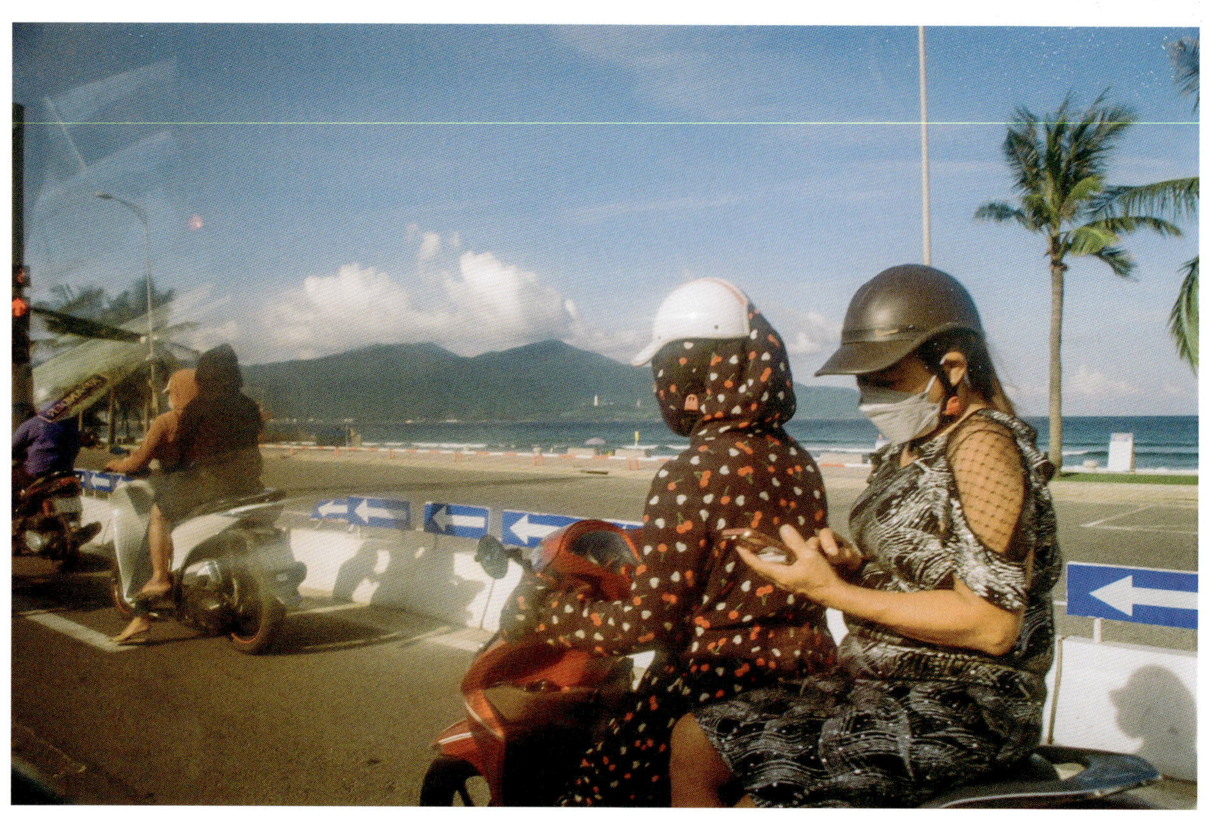

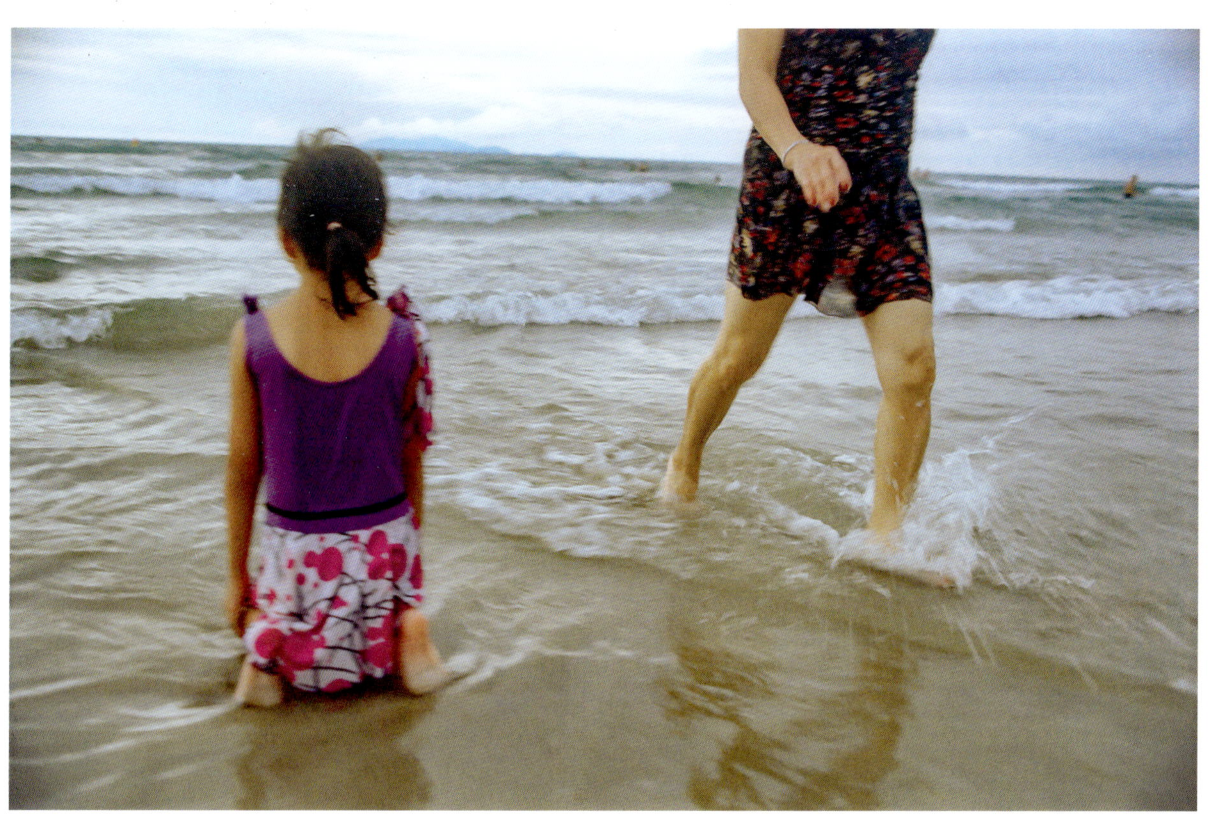

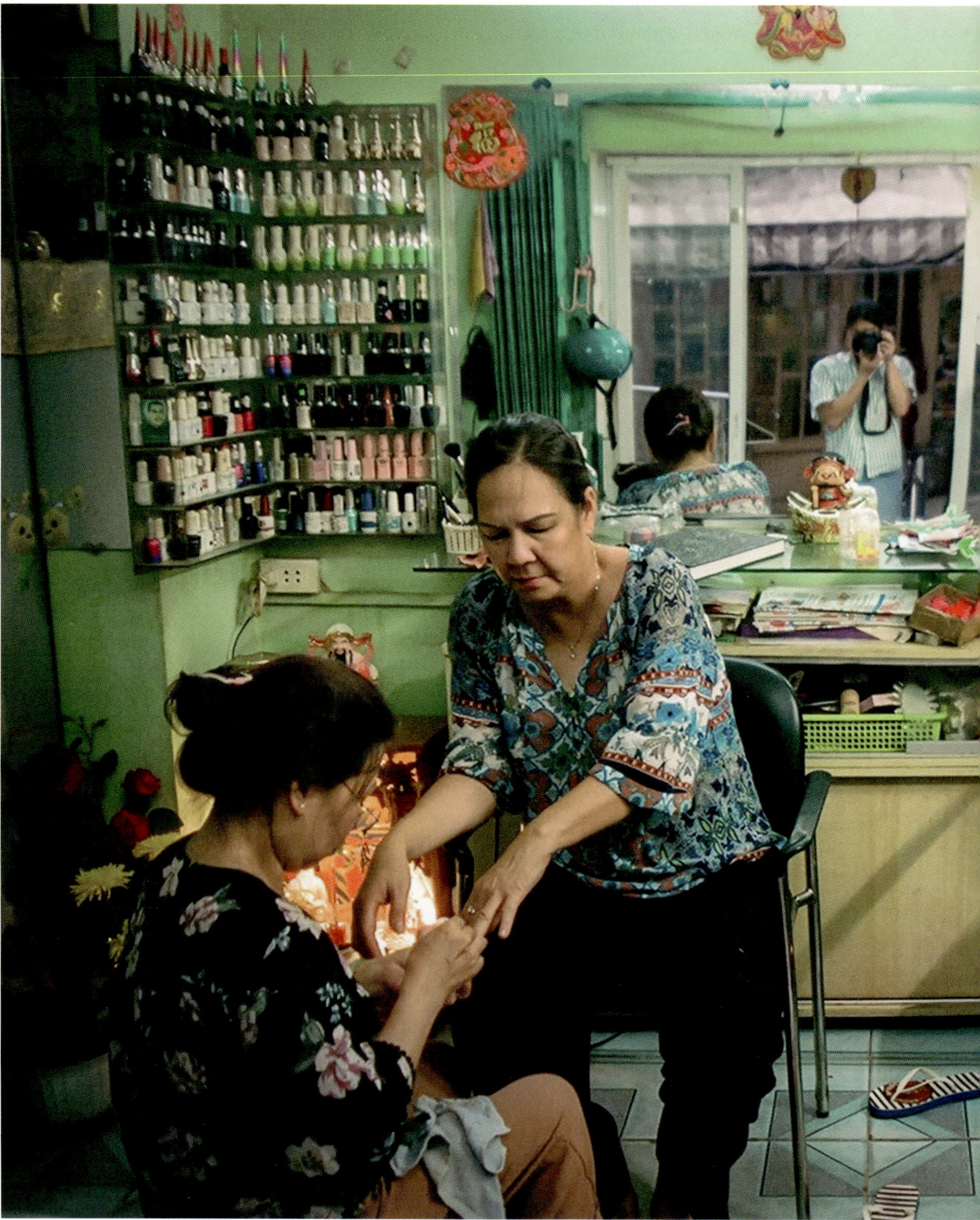

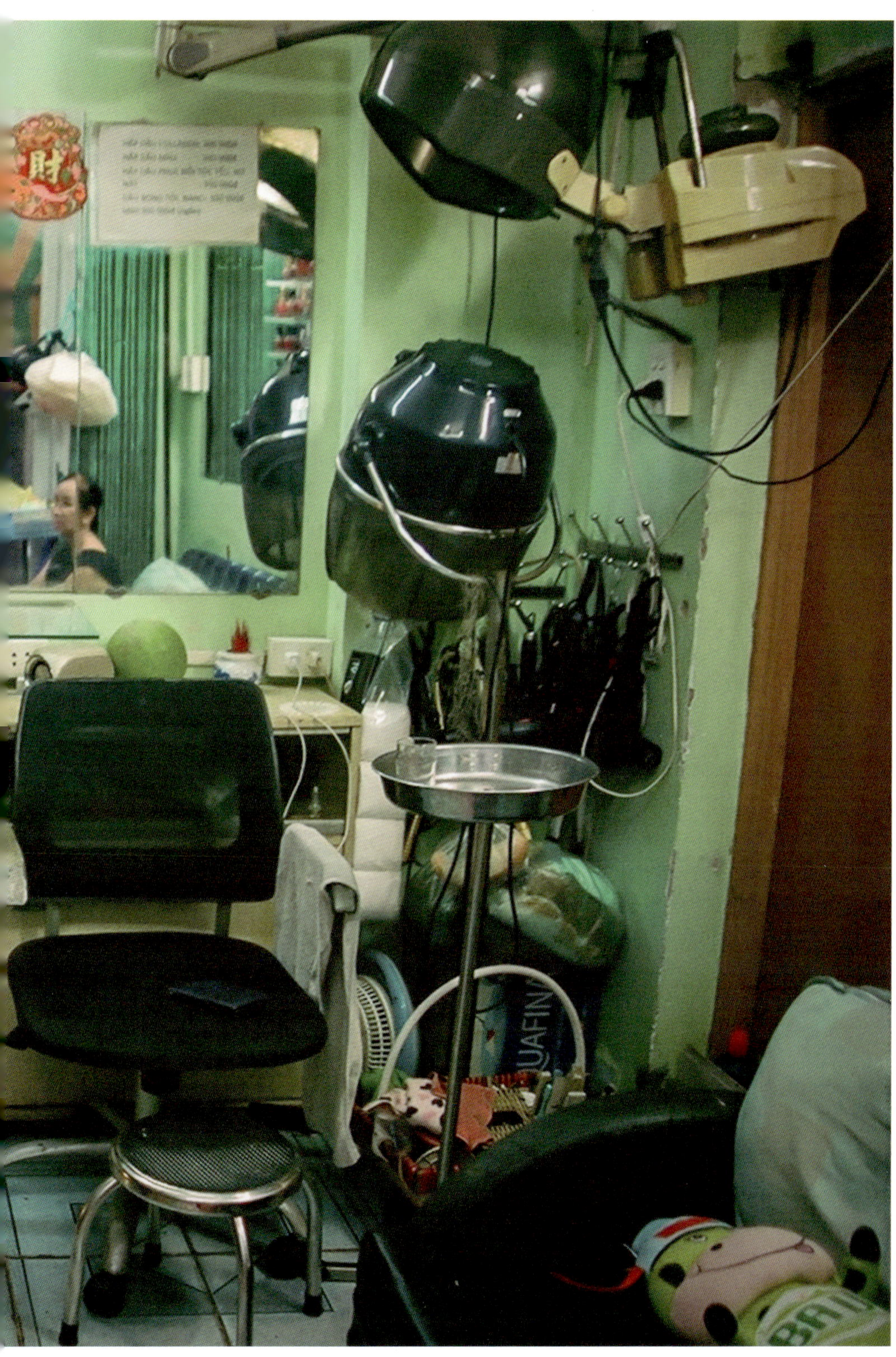

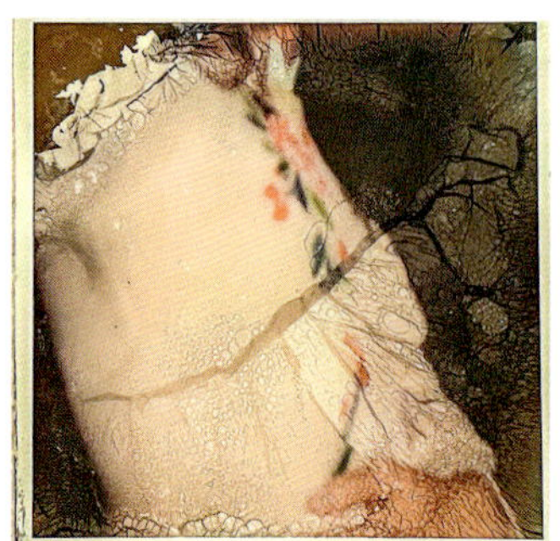
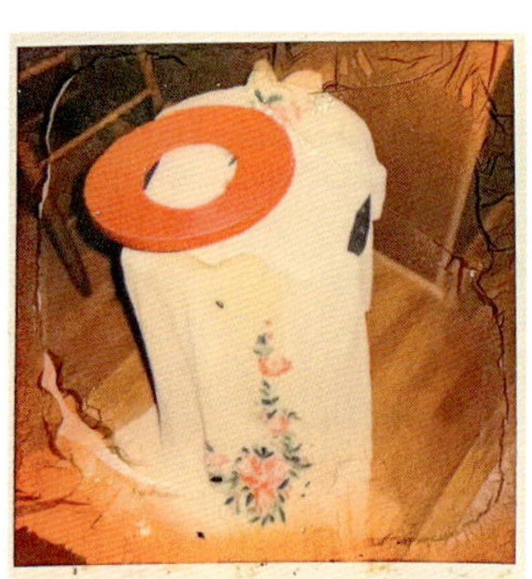
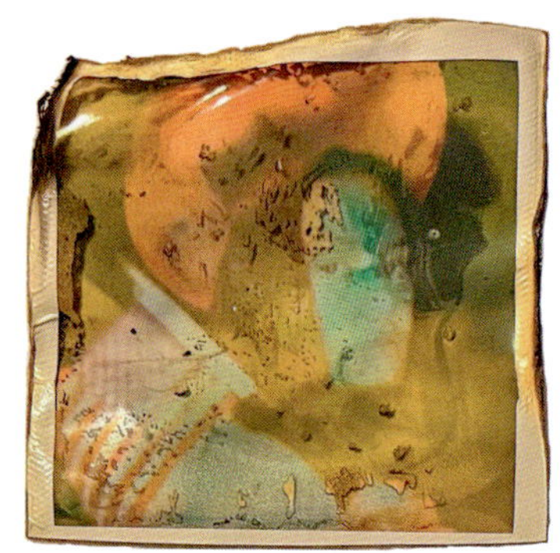
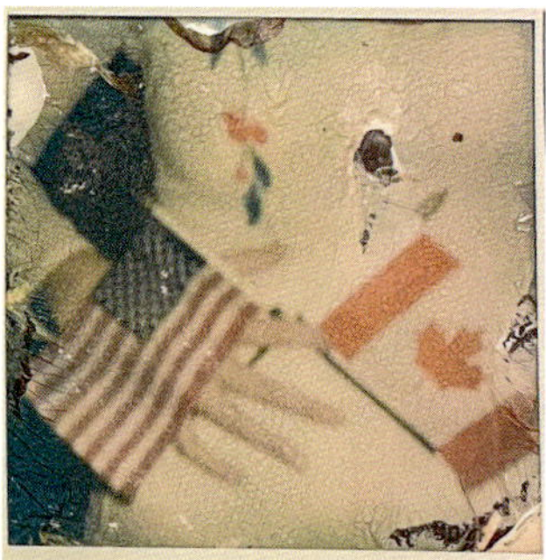
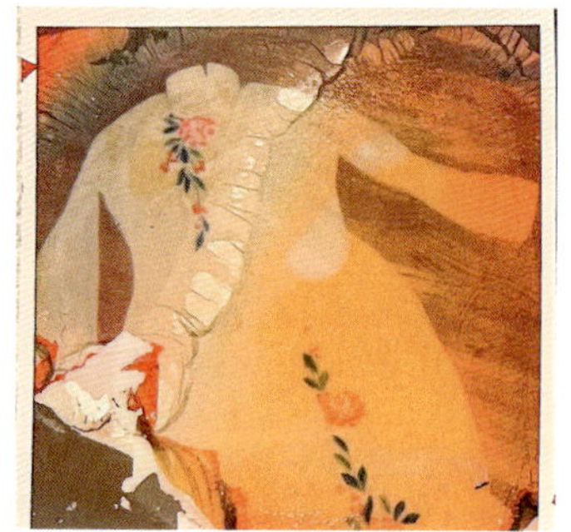

WHAT DOESN'T GO TOGETHER, COMES TOGETHER
SHIMMERING, MURKY BLOODLINES REACHING
A PENT-UP FRENZY
SUBMERGED IN DISORIENTING BLISS
DROWNED OUT BY ANGUISHED RAPTURE
BUT NOT UN-SETTLING
I CAN'T TELL YET IF I'M BUOYANT OR ERODED
I WISH TO DESTROY AND TRANSFORM MYSELF
EVERY OTHER DAY
WRAPPED IN A WET BLANKET OF PATRIOTISM
A BUBBLY AND PECULIAR FACELIFT
NEW BLOOD RUSH; THE DECK HAS SHUFFLED
I WILL NEVER BE TRAPPED IN YOUR
CITIZENSHIP BUT I WILL CRADLE HER GRAVE
I WILL FORGET THEIR NAMES BUT I WILL
NEVER FORGET HER PAIN

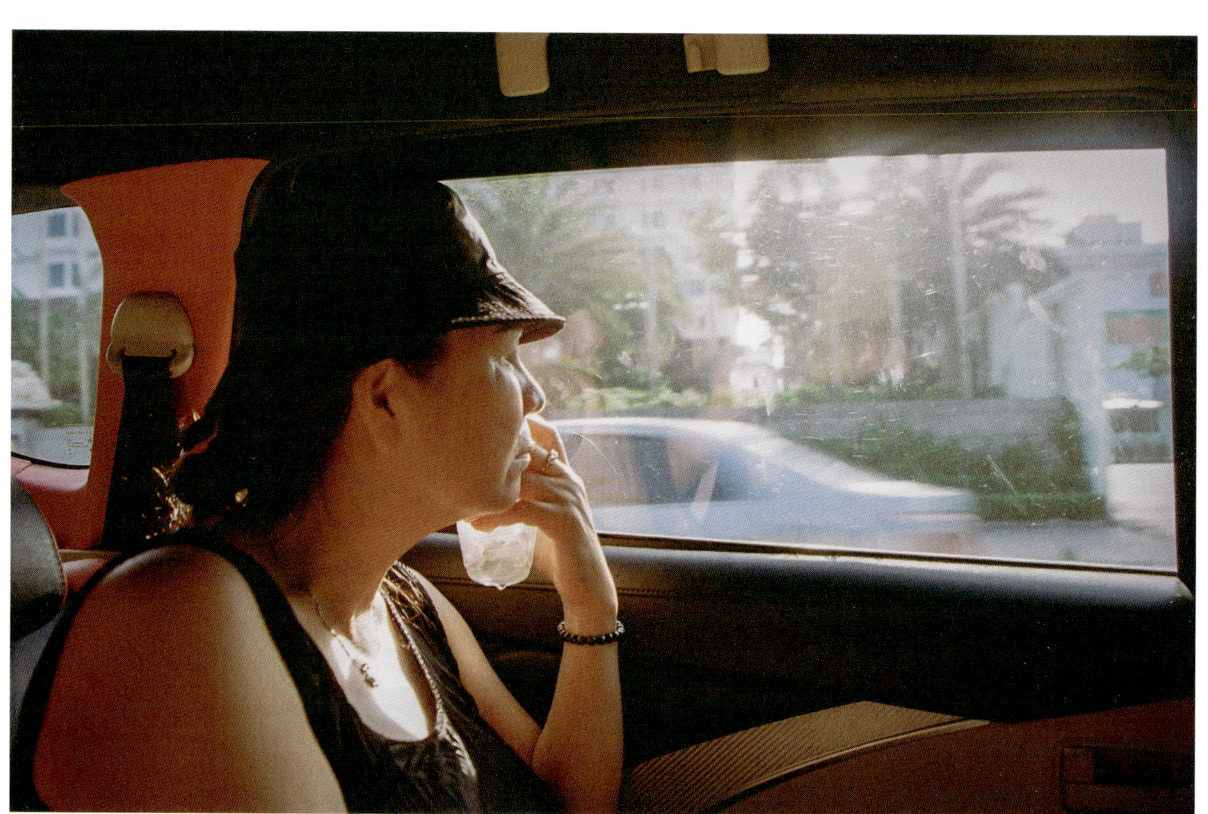

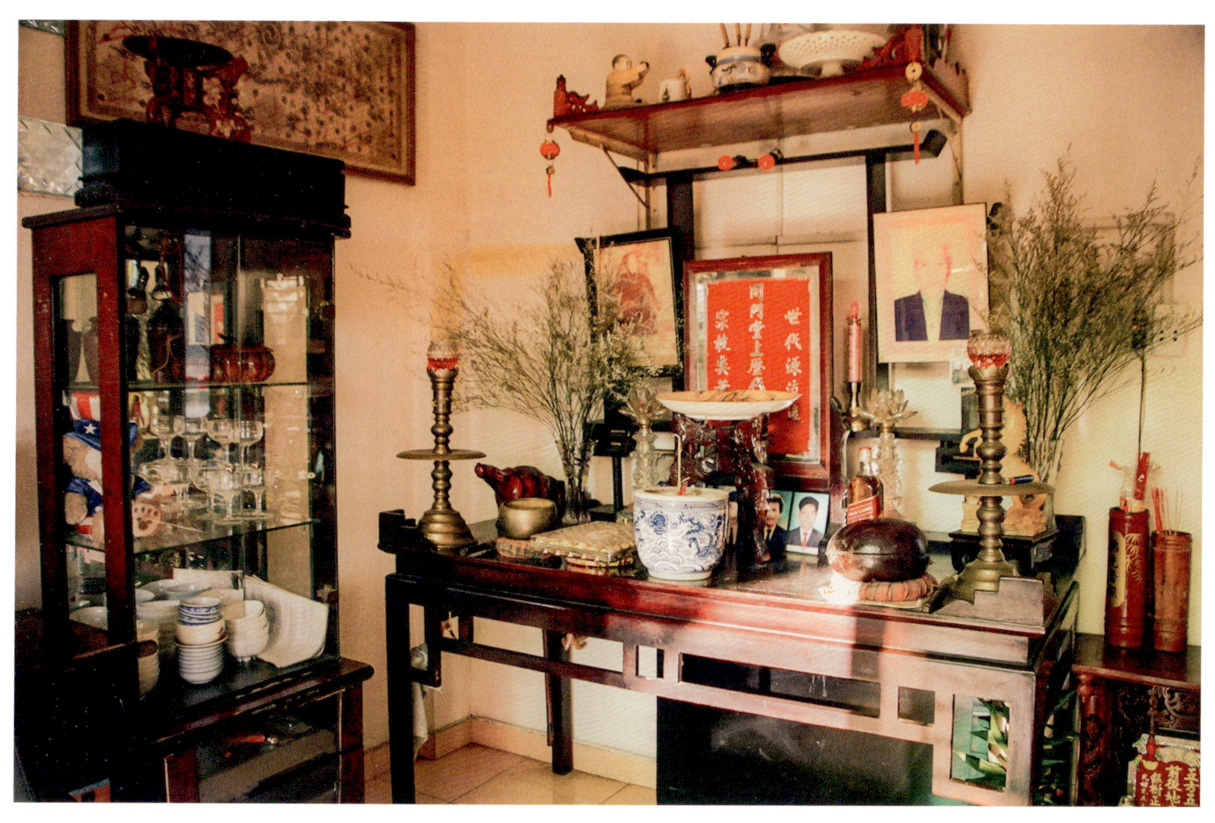

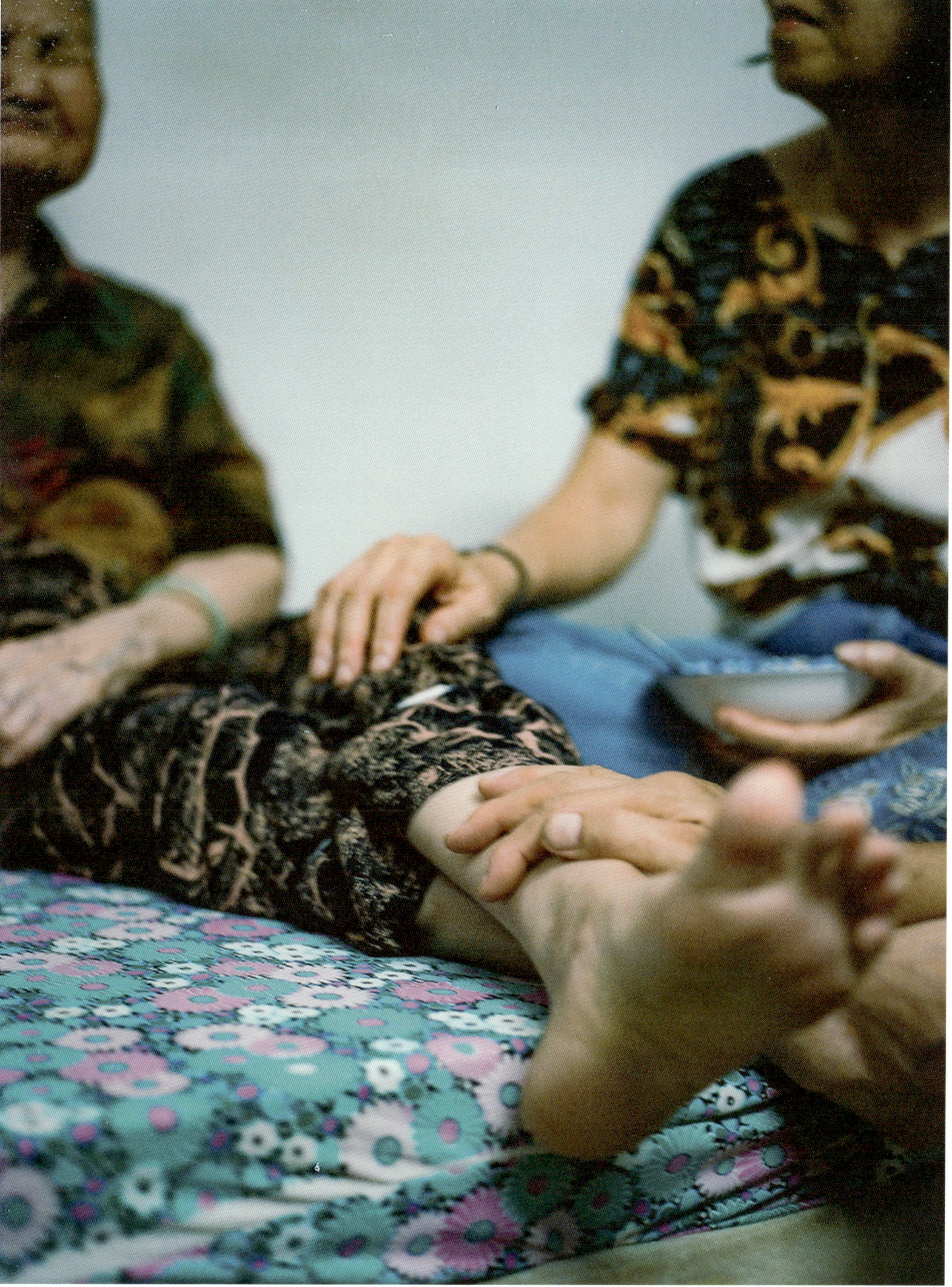

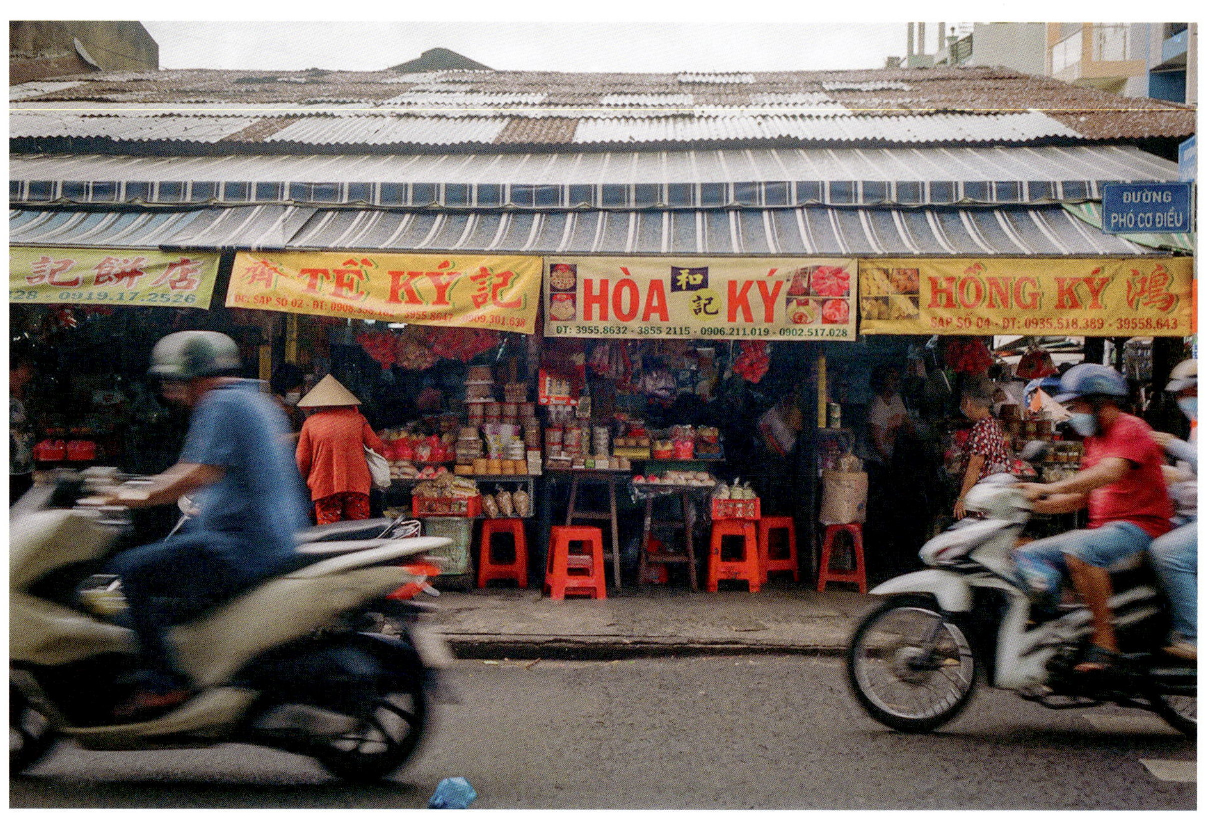
記餅店
0919.17.2526
齋 TẾ KÝ 記
HÒA 和 記 KÝ
ĐT: 3955.8632 - 3855 2115 - 0906.211.019 - 0902.517.028
HỒNG KÝ 鴻
SẠP SỐ 04 - ĐT: 0935.518.389 - 39558.643
ĐƯỜNG
PHÓ CƠ ĐIỀU

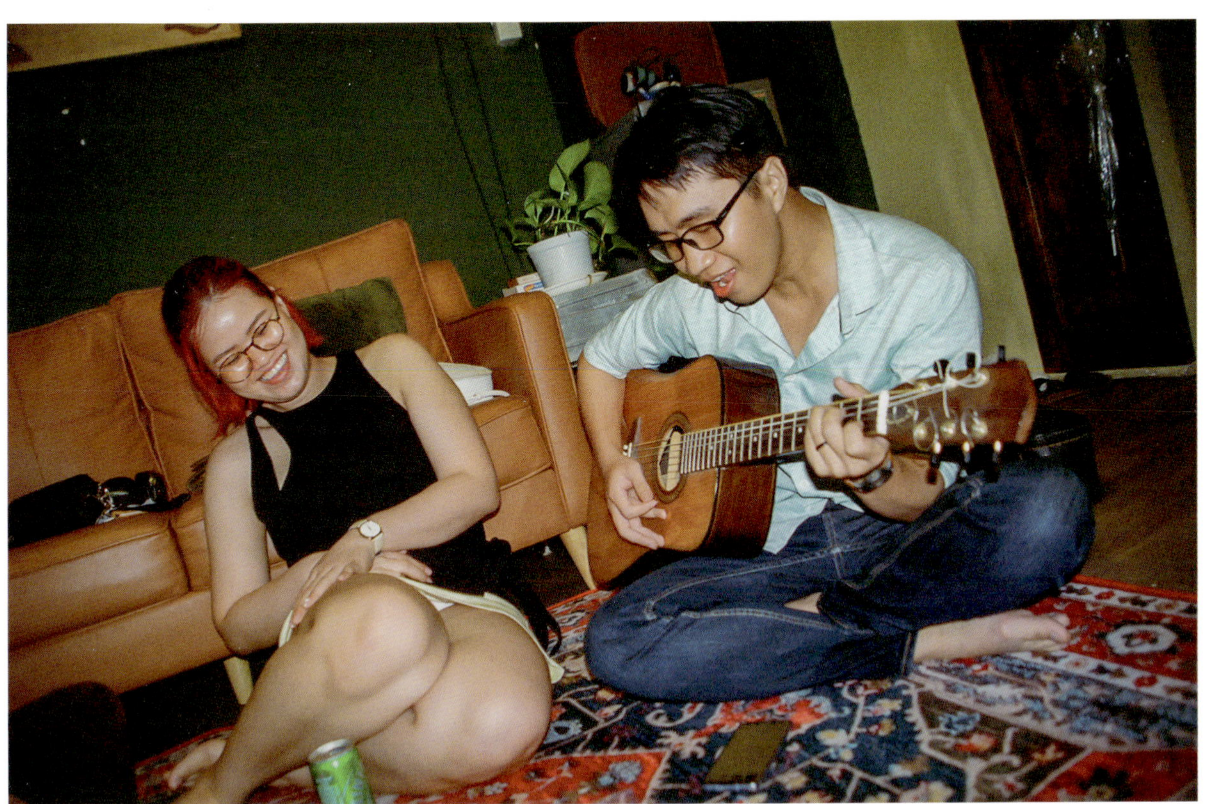

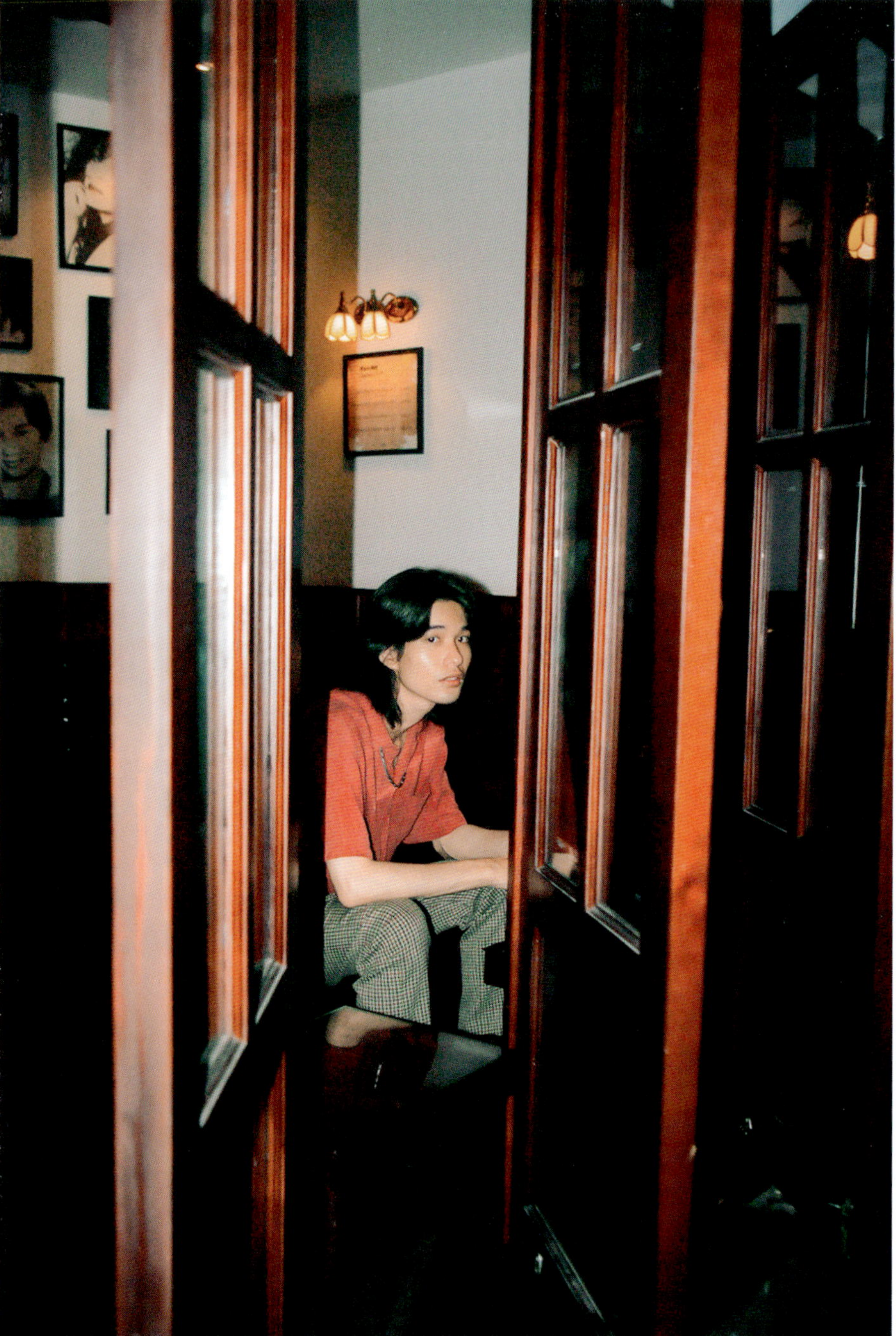

Sep. 30, 2022

Tomorrow is my last day in Vietnam. I have been here for 2 weeks and I've only been able to write 3 times. I guess it's been way too physically and emotionally draining that I haven't been able to process how this trip is affecting me. It's been 12 years since I've been back in Vietnam. I was 16 the last time I was here. A completely different person. COVID has made it hard to visit in recent years, but this was a trip long overdue and we finally made it happen. The time spent away and distance from my homeland has made this trip difficult. Because now it is too much. I cried and cried and cried last night. I bonded with 5 of my cousins last night at Uncle Thuc's house. I had to learn and re-learn their names. Something strange yet delightful happened - I felt something so incredibly heavy, so indelible, hard to explain. everything I've seen from the movies and from friends that I've yearned for. Unconditional family love. Love from the basic and fundamental reason of sharing family blood. To hear that someone will drop everything and care for me "because you're my cousin" is foreign yet everything I want to hear. I'm falling back in love with where I came from yet crushed with guilt. Cleansed, washed burnt, transfigured - from everything I've gained and from losing what I thought I knew. By being here I am letting Saigon fracture and heal by telling me its story.

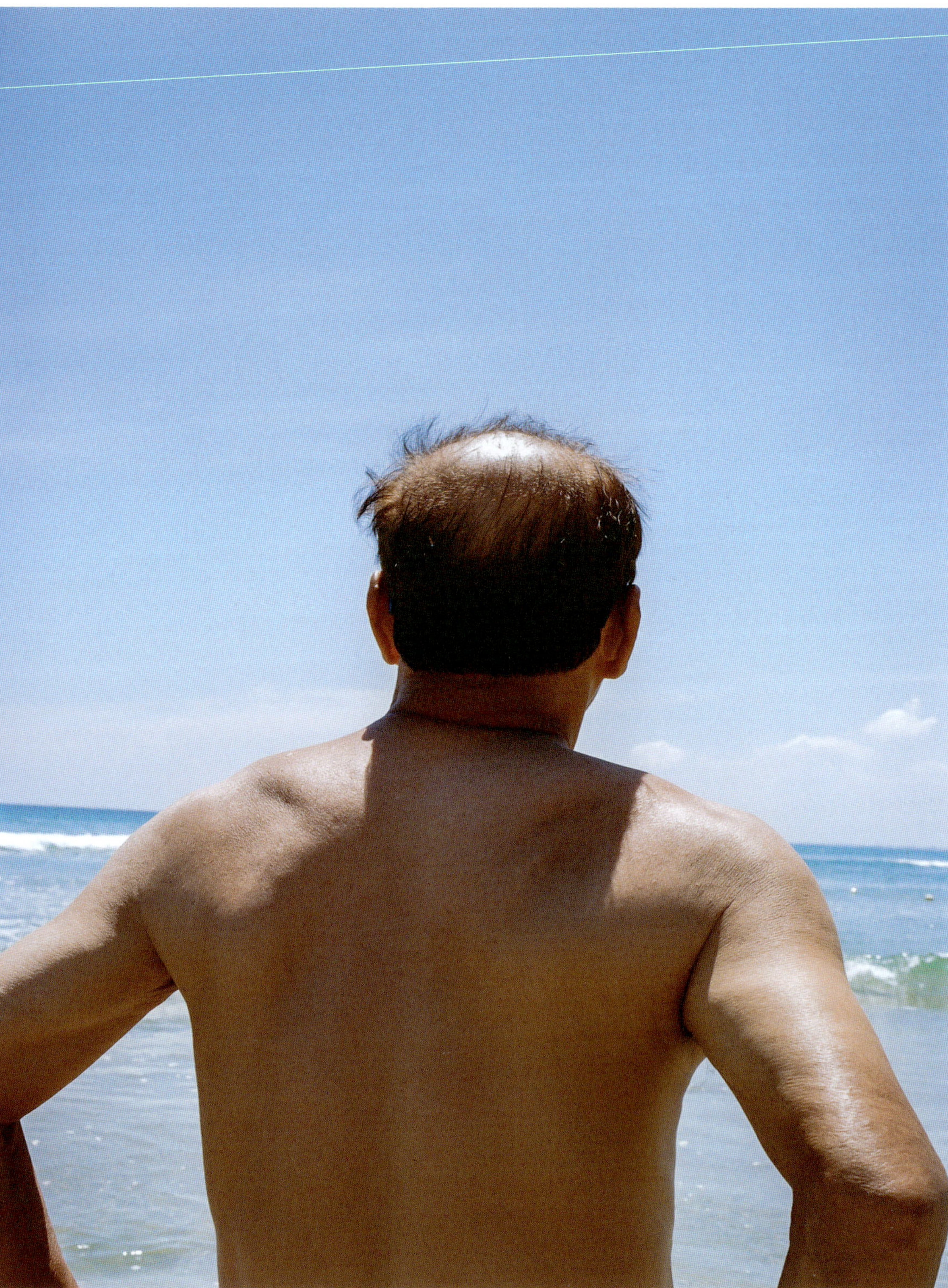

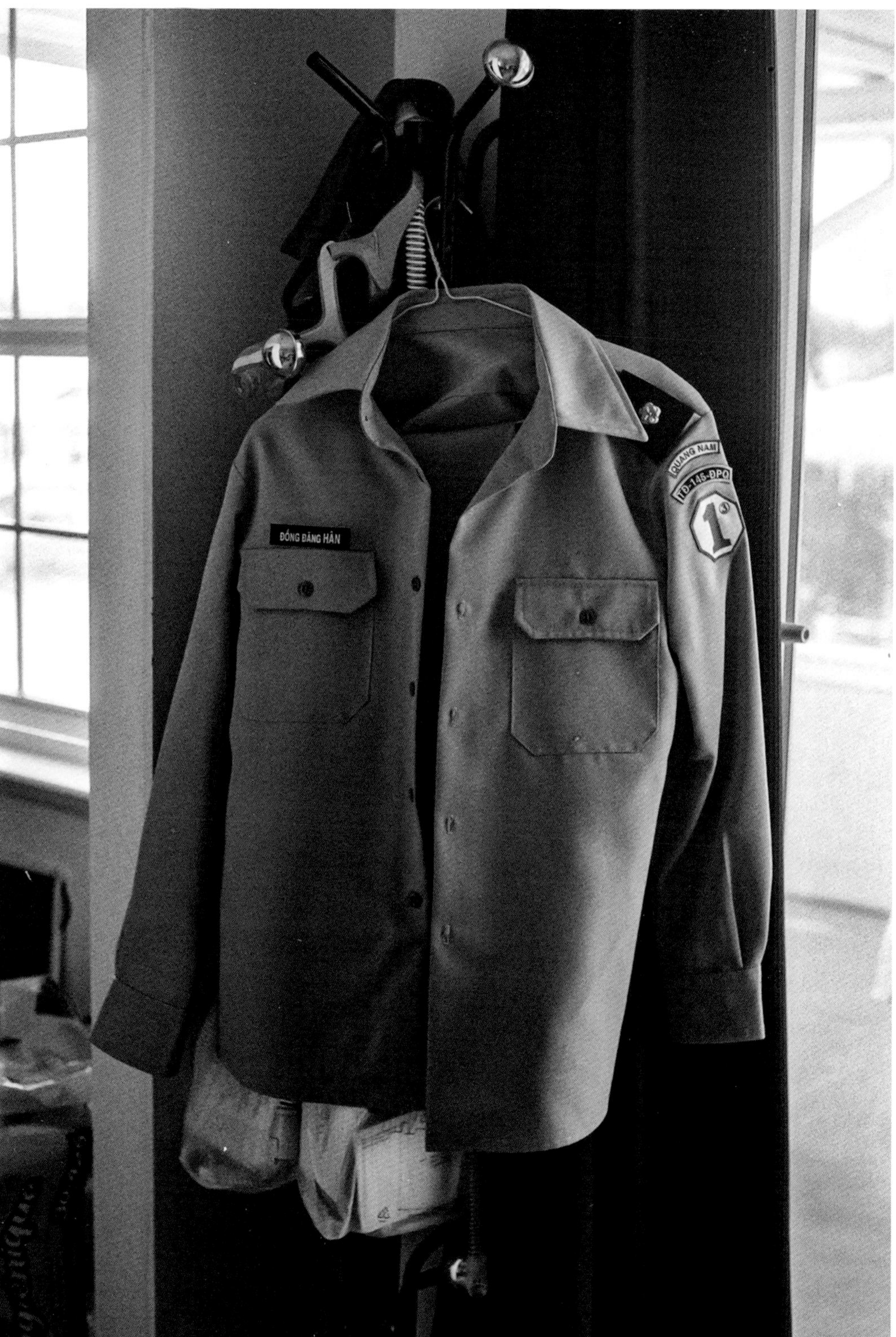
ĐỒNG ĐĂNG HÂN
QUANG NAM
TĐ-145-ĐPQ
1